D0517824

The Microwave Cookbook

Contents

PRECAUTIONS TO AVOID POSSIBLE EXPOSURE TO EXCESSIVE MICROWAVE ENERGY

(a) Do not attempt to operate this oven with the door open since open-door operation can result in harmful exposure to microwave energy. It is important not to defeat or tamper with the safety interlocks.

(b) Do not place any object between the oven front face and the door or allow soil or cleaner residue to accumulate on sealing surfaces.

(c) Do not operate the oven if it is damaged. It is particularly important that the oven door close properly and that there is no damage to the:
  (1) door (bent)
  (2) hinges and latches (broken or loosened)
  (3) door seals and sealing surfaces

(d) The oven should not be adjusted or repaired by anyone except properly qualified service personnel.

◄ *Chicken A La Roma; for recipe, see page 41.*

Microwave Techniques

The characteristics of food and the application of certain techniques will influence the speed and effectiveness of microwave cooking. While the techniques may be familiar, the way they are used may be somewhat different because of the unique way in which microwave energy cooks.

STARTING TEMPERATURE Suggested cook times in this book are based on normal storage temperatures. Foods which are refrigerated or frozen may require longer cooking time than foods stored at room temperature.

DENSITY In both conventional and microwave cooking, dense foods, such as potatoes, take longer to cook or reheat than light porous foods such as a piece of cake, bread or a roll.

MOISTURE CONTENT Moisture of food affects how it cooks. Very moist foods cook evenly because microwave energy is attracted to water molecules. Food with low moisture content should be covered during cooking and allowed to stand after cooking so heat can disperse evenly.

QUANTITY In microwave cooking, where time is directly related to the number of servings, small amounts of food take less time to cook than large ones.

SIZE Foods which are similar in size and shape cook more evenly. Small pieces cook faster than large ones. When cooking large pieces of food such as a roast, the power level may be reduced to allow for more even cooking.

STIRRING When microwaving, for best results, stir foods from the outside to the center of the dish once or twice during cooking. Foods which require constant stirring conventionally will need only occasional stirring. When possible, stir foods before serving.

ROTATING Repositioning a dish in the oven may help foods cook evenly. To rotate ½ turn, turn the dish until the side which was to the back of the oven is to the front. To rotate ¼ turn, turn the dish until the side which was to the back of the oven is to the side.

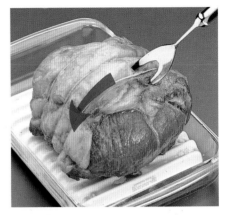

TURNING OVER When microwaving, turning over or rearranging is often needed to allow for even heating of foods. Turning large cuts of meat or frozen hamburgers over once or twice during cooking will give best results.

STAND TIME In microwaving, stand time is necessary to allow foods to finish cooking. During stand time, moist surface areas on cakes will disappear and the internal temperature of a roast will continue to rise. Most recipes require stand times ranging from 5 to 15 minutes.

TEMPERATURE Foods with delicate textures are best cooked at lower power levels. Using the temperature probe can prevent milk-based liquids from over cooking. To ensure thorough heating, foods should reach a temperature of 160°F to 165°F before serving.

DO NOT MICROWAVE. Do not cook eggs in shells. Avoid heating foods in narrow necked jars and bottles. Always remove lids from wide necked jars before warming food. Heating baby food in jars is not recommended.

PRICK FOODS TO RELEASE PRESSURE. Steam causes pressure to build in foods which are tightly covered by a skin or membrane. Prick potatoes, egg yolks and chicken livers to prevent bursting.

ARRANGEMENT Place individual items, like custard cups or baked potatoes in a ring. Allow space between foods so energy can penetrate from all sides.

SHIELDING When microwave cooking or defrosting, foods may be shielded to prevent overcooking. Use small strips of foil to shield thin parts, such as the tips of wings and legs on poultry, which may cook before larger parts.

SHAPE OF FOOD When microwaving, arrange foods with the thickest or less tender portions to the outside of the dish. This prevents thinner more tender pieces from overcooking. Arrange foods of equal size in a ring, leaving the center empty.

COVERING To cook quickly and retain moisture, cover dish with a lid or plastic wrap. Vent plastic wrap by turning back one edge to form a narrow slot where excess steam can escape. To hold in heat and prevent spatters without steaming, use wax paper.

POROUS COVERS Paper towels or napkins allow steam to escape, absorb moisture and prevent spattering. For best results wrap food such as breads and baking items in a paper towel or napkin.

Microwaves pass through paper, glass, plastic and ceramic utensils. These materials are ideal for microwave oven cooking because they allow microwave energy to penetrate the food. Paper towels and napkins absorb moisture in foods like bacon and aid in retaining moisture in foods such as breads and rolls.

Microwaves are reflected by metal. Foil wrapped boxes, aluminum containers deeper than ¾ inch, metal baking utensils and conventional meat thermometers are not suitable for use in microwave ovens. Do not use glass, pottery or pyroceram utensils with metal trim or fittings.

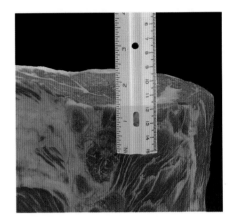

Microwaves penetrate to a depth of about ¾ to 1¼ inches. This microwave energy causes molecules within the food to vibrate, producing the heat necessary to cook the food.

Foods should be arranged with the meatiest portions around the outer edge of the dish and thinner pieces towards the middle. This enables thick portions to cook completely without overcooking thin pieces.

Size and shape of a container will influence the microwave cooking time. A shallow casserole exposes more food surface to microwave energy and will require less time to cook than taller utensils holding the same amount. Since microwaves penetrate from all sides, round shapes and rings cook more evenly.

Today many convenience foods are packaged in containers designed especially for use in microwave ovens. Consult package instructions for cooking procedures.

Defrosting Techniques

See Pages 118-119 For Defrosting Chart.

Casseroles, soups and stews will require stirring once or twice during defrosting. Layered casseroles that cannot be stirred, such as lasagna, should be rotated several times to allow for more even defrosting.

Remove meat from the original wrapper and place in baking dish. After first half of defrosting time, break up or separate ground beef, steaks, chops, chicken pieces or fish fillets. Remove any defrosted pieces and return remainder to oven to continue defrosting. If additional thawing is needed, return frozen portions to oven to complete defrosting.

Turn large roasts, whole chickens and cornish hens over after half of defrosting time. Shield warm areas with small pieces of foil. For whole poultry, start with the breast side down; shield legs and wing tips after turning over. Defrost meats and poultry only until they can be pierced to the center with a skewer. The surface should feel cool but not icy.

Microwave Oven Wattage

All microwave ovens have similar components but the wattage (power output) will vary. Larger models offer between 700 and 1000 watts of cooking power. Compact models yield less — usually 500 to 600 watts. The lower the wattage, the longer it will take food to cook.

To determine the wattage of your oven, check the Use and Care Book or the oven nameplate. If the information is not available, use this easy test to measure the wattage. In a 2-cup glass measure, heat 1 cup of tap water at High power. If the water boils in less than 3 minutes, your oven probably has 600 or more watts.

All of the recipes in this book have been tested in 700 to 1000 watt ovens. If your microwave oven has less than 700 watts of power output, cooking times may be longer.

Recipe Analysis

Calories per serving and a nutrient analysis are provided for each recipe. The nutrients listed include grams of protein, fat and carbohydrate in addition to milligrams of cholesterol and sodium.

These calorie and nutrient values are obtained from computer analysis, based primarily on information from the U.S. Department of Agriculture. The values are as accurate as possible and are

based on the following guidelines:

• All nutrient breakdowns are listed per serving.
• When a range is given for an ingredient (for example, 2 to 2½ cups), the smaller amount is calculated.
• When a marinade is given, only the amount of marinade actually used (not discarded) is calculated.
• Garnishes and other optional ingredients are not included in the calculation.
• Fruits and vegetables listed in the ingredients are not peeled unless specified.
• Calculations apply only to the original recipe and not to any accompanying variations.

Microwave Adapting

When adapting recipes for the microwave, it is best to start with a familiar recipe. Knowing how the food should look and taste will help when adapting it for microwaving. Foods that require browning or crisp, dry surfaces will cook best in a conventional oven.

- Refer to similar microwave recipes for cooking techniques, power levels and microwaving time.

- Moist foods such as vegetables, fruits, poultry and seafood microwave well.

- Rich foods such as bar cookies, moist cakes and candies are suitable for microwaving because of their high fat and sugar content.

- Reduce conventional cooking time by one-third to one-half. Check food after minimum time to avoid overcooking.

- Small amounts of butter or oil can be used for flavoring but are not needed to prevent sticking.

- Seasonings may need to be reduced. Salt meats and vegetables after cooking.

- Liquids may need to be reduced.

Recipe Conversion

Conventional Spanish Rice

1 lb. ground beef
1 (28 oz.) can whole tomatoes, cut up
1½ cups water
¾ cup long grain rice
2 tablespoons chili powder
2 tablespoons instant minced onion
1 teaspoon salt
⅛ teaspoon pepper

In 10-in. skillet, crumble ground beef. Cook over medium high heat 10 minutes, uncovered. Add tomatoes, water, rice, chili powder, onion, salt and pepper. Mix well. Cover and cook over medium heat 35 to 40 minutes.

Total Cooking Time 45 to 50 Minutes
Serves 4 to 6

Microwave Spanish Rice

1 lb. ground chuck
1 (28 oz.) can whole tomatoes, cut up
1 cup instant rice
2 tablespoons chili powder
1 tablespoon instant minced onion
1 teaspoon salt
⅛ teaspoon pepper

In 2-quart casserole, crumble beef. Add tomatoes, rice, chili powder, minced onions, salt and pepper. Mix well. Cover. Microwave at HIGH (10) 11 to 14 minutes, stirring after 6 minutes. If top of food appears dry during cooking, stir again. Return to oven to finish cooking.

Total Cooking Time 11 to 14 Minutes
Serves 4 to 6

CONVENTIONAL   **MICROWAVE**

Appetizers & Beverages

Garlic Shrimp

2 tablespoons butter
2 cloves garlic, minced
¼ lb. fresh medium shrimp, peeled and deveined
1½ teaspoons fresh parsley, snipped
1½ teaspoons grated Parmesan cheese

In small mixing bowl, combine butter and garlic. Microwave at HIGH (10) 1 to 2 minutes. Add shrimp and parsley. Microwave at MEDIUM HIGH (7) 1 to 2 minutes; stir after 30 seconds. Stir in Parmesan cheese. Yield: 4 servings (165 calories each).

Total Microwave Cooking Time 2 to 4 Minutes

PROTEIN 21.6 / FAT 7.8 / CARBOHYDRATE 1.1 / SODIUM 225 / CHOLESTEROL 175

Oriental Meatballs

1 lb. lean ground beef
½ lb. ground pork
½ cup canned water chestnuts, drained, finely chopped
¼ cup green pepper, finely chopped
3 green onions, chopped
¼ teaspoon salt
2 tablespoons soy sauce
2 tablespoons pineapple juice

Sauce:
1 (20 oz.) can pineapple chunks
1 tablespoon instant beef bouillon granules
¼ cup brown sugar, packed
2 tablespoons cornstarch
1 tablespoon soy sauce
2 tablespoons vinegar
½ cup water

In large mixing bowl, combine beef, pork, water chestnuts, green pepper, onions, salt, soy sauce and pineapple juice; mix well. Shape into 1-inch meatballs. Arrange in 2-quart oblong glass baking dish. Cover with wax paper. Microwave at HIGH (10) 9 to 13 minutes until meat is thoroughly cooked; rearrange after 6 minutes. Drain meatballs and set aside.

Drain pineapple, reserving liquid. In 4-cup glass measure, combine reserved pineapple juice, beef bouillon, brown sugar, cornstarch, soy sauce, vinegar and water. Microwave at HIGH (10) 3 to 5 minutes, until mixture thickens; stir after 2 minutes. Add pineapple. Pour sauce over meatballs. Microwave at HIGH (10) 2 to 3 minutes until heated through. Yield: 50 meatballs (63 calories each).

Total Microwave Cooking Time 14 to 21 Minutes

PROTEIN 3.1 / FAT 3.7 / CARBOHYDRATE 4.5 / SODIUM 94 / CHOLESTEROL 13

Cheese Ball

¼ cup butter
1 (3 oz.) pkg. cream cheese
1 teaspoon Worcestershire sauce
½ teaspoon onion powder
⅛ teaspoon garlic powder
3 cups Cheddar cheese, shredded
½ cup walnuts, finely chopped or fresh parsley, snipped
Assorted crackers

Place butter in 1-cup glass measure. Microwave at HIGH (10) 15 to 20 seconds until butter softens. Place cream cheese in 2-quart glass mixing bowl. Microwave at MEDIUM (5) 45 seconds to 1 minute until cream cheese softens. Blend in softened butter, Worcestershire sauce, onion powder, garlic powder and Cheddar cheese. Beat at medium speed of electric mixer until smooth. Shape into ball. Roll in nuts or parsley to coat. Refrigerate for 3 hours. Serve with crackers. Yield: one 4-inch cheese ball (44 calories per tablespoon).

Total Microwave Cooking Time 1 Minute To 1 Minute 20 Seconds

◀ *Garlic Shrimp*

PROTEIN 1.8 / FAT 4.0 / CARBOHYDRATE 0.3 / SODIUM 51 / CHOLESTEROL 10

Appetizers & Beverages

▲ *Vegetable Crispers, Taco Chicken Wingettes and Cocktail Reubens*

Vegetable Crispers

Place buttered vegetables into plastic bag with crumb mixture and shake to coat evenly.

¾ **cup dry bread crumbs**
¾ **cup grated Parmesan cheese**
1 **teaspoon tarragon leaves, crushed**
1 **teaspoon paprika**
¼ **teaspoon salt**
Dash pepper
1 **cup broccoli flowerets**
1 **cup cauliflower flowerets**
1 **medium zucchini, sliced ½-inch thick**
12 **small whole mushrooms**
½ **cup butter, melted**

Combine bread crumbs, Parmesan cheese, tarragon, paprika, salt and pepper in plastic bag. Taking several pieces at a time, dip broccoli, cauliflower, zucchini and mushrooms in melted butter. Place into plastic bag with crumb mixture and shake to coat evenly. Repeat until all vegetables are coated. Arrange in single layer in 2-quart oblong glass baking dish. Cover with paper towel. Microwave at HIGH (10) 3 to 5 minutes until tender. Some vegetables may cook faster than others. Remove vegetables as they become tender. Serve warm. Yield: 40 appetizers (39 calories each).

Total Microwave Cooking Time 3 to 5 Minutes

PROTEIN 1.3 / FAT 2.9 / CARBOHYDRATE 2.4 / SODIUM 83 / CHOLESTEROL 7

Taco Chicken Wingettes

2 lbs. chicken wings
  (about 10)
1½ cups cornflake crumbs
1 teaspoon chili powder
½ teaspoon cumin
¼ teaspoon cayenne
¼ teaspoon garlic powder
½ cup butter, melted

Remove wing tips from chicken; discard. Cut each wing at joint to make 2 sections. Set aside.

Combine cornflake crumbs, chili powder, cumin, cayenne and garlic powder in plastic bag. Dip chicken pieces in melted butter. Place in plastic bag with crumb mixture and shake to coat evenly. Arrange in a single layer in a 2-quart oblong glass baking dish. Cover with wax paper. Microwave at HIGH (10) 8 to 10 minutes. Serve warm. Yield: 10 appetizers (168 calories each).

Total Microwave Cooking Time 8 to 10 Minutes

PROTEIN 7.3 / FAT 10.3 / CARBOHYDRATE 11.2 / SODIUM 277 / CHOLESTEROL 41

Cocktail Reubens

36 slices cocktail rye bread,
  toasted
½ cup Thousand Island
  dressing
1 (8 oz.) can sauerkraut,
  rinsed and drained
¼ lb. thinly-sliced corned
  beef
1 (6 oz.) pkg. Swiss cheese
  slices, each slice cut into
  4 squares

Arrange 9 slices of bread on paper towel lined plate. Spread each slice with about ¾ teaspoon Thousand Island dressing. Add small amount of sauerkraut and corned beef to each slice. Top each with 1 square Swiss cheese. Microwave at MEDIUM HIGH (7) 2 to 3 minutes until cheese melts. Repeat with remaining ingredients. Yield: 36 appetizers (100 calories each).

Total Microwave Cooking Time 2 to 3 Minutes

PROTEIN 4.3 / FAT 3.3 / CARBOHYDRATE 14.0 / SODIUM 260 / CHOLESTEROL 9

Seaside Cheese Dip

1 (6½ oz.) can minced
  clams
2 (5 oz.) jars sharp Cheddar
  cheese spread, softened
1 (8 oz.) pkg. cream cheese,
  softened
1 tablespoon Worcestershire
  sauce
½ medium green pepper,
  chopped
2 green onions, chopped

Drain clams, reserving ¼ cup liquid. In 1½-quart casserole, combine drained clams, reserved clam juice, sharp Cheddar cheese spread, cream cheese, Worcestershire sauce, green pepper and onions. Microwave at MEDIUM (5) 6 to 9 minutes; stir after 4 minutes. Yield: 1½ cups (44 calories per tablespoon).

Total Microwave Cooking Time 6 to 9 Minutes

PROTEIN 2.0 / FAT 3.5 / CARBOHYDRATE 1.1 / SODIUM 142 / CHOLESTEROL 12

Appetizers & Beverages

▲ *Spicy Taco Spread*

Spicy Taco Spread

1 lb. lean ground beef
1 small onion, chopped
⅓ cup green pepper, chopped
3 jalapeno peppers, seeded and chopped
½ teaspoon chili powder
½ teaspoon oregano
½ teaspoon cumin
¼ teaspoon thyme
1 (6 oz.) can tomato paste
1 teaspoon Worcestershire sauce
½ teaspoon chili powder
¼ teaspoon cumin
Dash cayenne pepper
2 (8 oz.) pkgs. cream cheese
1 teaspoon parsley flakes
½ teaspoon chili powder
1 cup lettuce, shredded
½ cup tomato, chopped

In a 1½-quart casserole, combine ground beef, onion, peppers, ½ teaspoon chili powder, oregano, ½ teaspoon cumin and thyme. Microwave at HIGH (10) 4 to 7 minutes, stirring every 2 minutes; drain. Add tomato paste, Worcestershire sauce, ½ teaspoon chili powder, ¼ teaspoon cumin and cayenne. Microwave at HIGH (10) 4 to 7 minutes, stirring after 3 minutes. Set aside. In 1-quart casserole, place cream cheese. Microwave at MEDIUM (5) 1 to 2 minutes; stir. Add parsley flakes and ½ teaspoon chili powder. Mix well. Spread cream cheese on large plate; add lettuce. Top with meat sauce and garnish with tomatoes. Serve with taco chips. Yield: 16 servings (193 calories per serving).

Total Microwave Cooking Time 9 to 16 Minutes

PROTEIN 6.6 / FAT 14.5 / CARBOHYDRATE 4.1 / SODIUM 112 / CHOLESTEROL 47

Shrimp-Stuffed Zucchini

4 small zucchini, cut into
    ¾-inch thick slices
1 tablespoon plus
    1½ teaspoons butter
¼ cup sweet red pepper,
    chopped
1 tablespoon all-purpose
    flour
¼ cup half & half
¼ cup onion, chopped
⅛ teaspoon salt
⅛ teaspoon white pepper
2 dashes hot sauce
1 (6 oz.) can tiny shrimp,
    rinsed and drained
Paprika

Scoop out center of each piece of zucchini to about halfway down on one end; set aside. Combine butter and red pepper in a 1-quart casserole. Microwave at HIGH (10) 1 to 2 minutes or until pepper is crisp-tender. Blend in flour. Gradually add half & half, stirring well. Stir in onion, salt, pepper and hot sauce. Microwave at HIGH (10) 1 minute or until thickened. Stir in shrimp.

Spoon 1 teaspoon shrimp mixture into each zucchini shell. Cover and chill thoroughly. Sprinkle with paprika before serving. Yield: 12 appetizer servings (46 calories each).

Total Microwave Cooking Time 2 to 3 Minutes

PROTEIN 4.0 / FAT 2.4 / CARBOHYDRATE 2.5 / SODIUM 67 / CHOLESTEROL 30

Scoop out center of each zucchini slice about halfway down on one end.

Artichoke Dip

1 (14 oz.) can artichoke
    hearts, drained and
    finely chopped
1 cup mayonnaise
1 cup grated Parmesan
    cheese
¼ teaspoon garlic salt
Paprika

In 8-inch square glass baking dish, mix chopped artichokes with mayonnaise, Parmesan cheese and garlic salt. Sprinkle with paprika. Microwave at HIGH (10) 3 to 5 minutes, until heated through; stir after 2 minutes. Yield: 2 cups (66 calories per tablespoon).

Total Microwave Cooking Time 3 to 5 Minutes

PROTEIN 1.4 / FAT 6.2 / CARBOHYDRATE 1.6 / SODIUM 110 / CHOLESTEROL 6

Party Mix

2 cups bite-size crispy corn
    squares
2 cups bite-size crispy rice
    squares
2 cups bite-size crispy
    wheat squares
1 cup salted peanuts
1 cup thin pretzel sticks
½ cup butter, melted
2 tablespoons
    Worcestershire sauce
¼ teaspoon garlic powder

In 2-quart oblong glass baking dish, combine corn squares, rice squares, wheat squares, peanuts and pretzel sticks; set aside. In 2-cup glass measure, blend melted butter, Worcestershire sauce and garlic powder. Pour butter mixture over cereals; stir until well coated. Microwave at HIGH (10) 4 to 7 minutes until butter is absorbed and mixture is crispy, stirring every 2 minutes. Cool before serving. Yield: 8 cups (450 calories per cup).

Choco-Peanut Party Mix: Prepare Party Mix as above, except add ½ cup creamy peanut butter to 4 tablespoons melted butter. Use only 1½ teaspoons Worcestershire sauce. After cooking, add 1 (8 oz.) pkg. candy coated chocolate pieces. Stir to mix.

Total Microwave Cooking Time 4 to 7 Minutes

PROTEIN 9.8 / FAT 21.4 / CARBOHYDRATE 57.0 / SODIUM 811 / CHOLESTEROL 31

Appetizers & Beverages

Hot Cheese Dip

¼ cup onion, finely
  chopped
1 tablespoon butter
1 teaspoon cornstarch
¼ teaspoon pepper
½ cup whipping cream
2 teaspoons Worcestershire
  sauce
1 teaspoon soy sauce
2 cups American cheese,
  shredded
1 (3 oz.) pkg. cream
  cheese, softened
2 teaspoons parsley,
  snipped
Assorted chips or vegetable
  dippers

In 1½-quart casserole, combine onion and butter. Microwave at HIGH (10) 1 to 2 minutes until onion is tender. Blend in cornstarch, pepper, cream, Worcestershire sauce and soy sauce. Microwave at HIGH (10) 2 to 3 minutes, until slightly thickened and bubbly, stirring every minute. Add American cheese, cream cheese and parsley. Microwave at HIGH (10) 2 to 4 minutes, until cheese is melted and mixture is heated through, stirring every minute. Yield: 2½ cups (42 calories per tablespoon).

Beer Cheese Dip: Prepare Hot Cheese Dip as above, substituting ¾ cup beer for cream.

Chili con Queso Dip: Prepare Hot Cheese Dip as above, substituting 1 cup shredded Monterey Jack cheese for 1 cup American cheese. Add 4 oz. can mild chopped green chili peppers and ⅛ teaspoon hot sauce when cheeses are added. Before serving, stir in 1 medium tomato, peeled, seeded and finely chopped.

Total Microwave Cooking Time 5 to 9 Minutes

PROTEIN 1.5 / FAT 3.9 / CARBOHYDRATE 0.5 / SODIUM 101 / CHOLESTEROL 13

Beef and Cheese Dip Aloha

1 (8 oz.) pkg. cream cheese
1 (2 ½ oz.) pkg. sliced
  dried beef,
  finely chopped
1 (8 oz.) can crushed
  pineapple, drained
¼ cup walnuts,
  coarsely chopped
¼ cup sour cream
2 tablespoons onion,
  finely chopped
2 tablespoons green pepper,
  finely chopped
2 tablespoons milk
½ teaspoon white pepper

Place cream cheese in 1-quart casserole. Microwave at MEDIUM (5) ¾ to 1 minute until softened. Add remaining ingredients and stir until well blended; cover. Microwave at MEDIUM (5) 3 to 5 minutes; stir once. Serve with melba toast rounds or unsalted crisp crackers. Yield: 2 cups (57 calories per tablespoon).

Total Microwave Cooking Time 3¾ to 6 Minutes

PROTEIN 1.9 / FAT 4.7 / CARBOHYDRATE 2.1 / SODIUM 133 / CHOLESTEROL 12

Sugar Glazed Walnuts

½ cup butter, melted
1 cup brown sugar, packed
1 teaspoon cinnamon
1 lb. walnut halves
  (about 4 cups)

In 1½-quart casserole, combine melted butter, brown sugar and cinnamon. Microwave at HIGH (10) 2 to 3 minutes; stir after 1 minute. Add nuts and mix to coat. Microwave at HIGH (10) 3 to 4 minutes. Spread on wax paper and cool slightly. Refrigerate in airtight container. Yield: 4 cups (584 calories per ½ cup).

Total Microwave Cooking Time 5 to 7 Minutes

PROTEIN 15.3 / FAT 46.9 / CARBOHYDRATE 34.3 / SODIUM 126 / CHOLESTEROL 31

Toasted Butter Pecans

1 lb. pecan halves
   (about 4 cups)
1 tablespoon seasoned salt
¼ cup butter

In 1½-quart casserole, place pecan halves. Sprinkle with seasoned salt. Cut butter into 4 pieces and arrange evenly over top. Microwave at HIGH (10) 4 to 6 minutes. Mix to distribute butter evenly. Serve warm or cold. Yield: 4 cups (413 calories per ½ cup).

Total Microwave Cooking Time 4 to 6 Minutes

PROTEIN 4.3 / FAT 42.3 / CARBOHYDRATE 10.2 / SODIUM 720 / CHOLESTEROL 16

Sweet-Tart Franks

1 (10 oz.) jar currant jelly
1 (6 oz.) jar Dijon mustard
2 lbs. frankfurters,
   cut into 1-inch pieces

In 2-quart casserole, combine jelly and mustard. Microwave at HIGH (10) 1 to 2 minutes until mixture can be stirred smooth. Add franks, stirring to coat each piece. Cover. Microwave at HIGH (10) 3½ to 6 minutes until franks are hot, stirring after 2 minutes. Serve immediately. Yield: 80 pieces (47 calories each).

Total Microwave Cooking Time 4½ to 8 Minutes

PROTEIN 1.3 / FAT 3.3 / CARBOHYDRATE 2.8 / SODIUM 177 / CHOLESTEROL 7

Spinach-Stuffed Mushrooms

12 large mushrooms (about
   2 inches in diameter)
1 (12 oz.) pkg. frozen
   spinach souffle
½ cup soft bread crumbs
1 teaspoon lemon juice
½ teaspoon instant
   minced onion
¼ teaspoon salt

Clean mushrooms and remove stems; set aside. With sharp knife cut souffle in half. Return half to freezer; place remaining half in 1-quart casserole. Microwave at HIGH (10) 4 to 5 minutes until partially defrosted. Mash with fork. Add crumbs, lemon juice, onion and salt; blend well.

Divide stuffing mixture evenly among mushroom caps. Arrange mushrooms in a circle on microwave-safe plate. Microwave at HIGH (10) 2 to 4 minutes or until hot. Yield: 12 appetizers (66 calories each).

Total Microwave Cooking Time 6 to 9 Minutes

PROTEIN 3.2 / FAT 4.1 / CARBOHYDRATE 4.5 / SODIUM 239 / CHOLESTEROL 38

Appetizers & Beverages

▲ *Wassail*

Wassail

1 quart apple cider
1 teaspoon allspice
½ teaspoon cloves
¼ teaspoon nutmeg
2 cinnamon sticks
½ cup orange juice
2 tablespoons lemon juice
½ cup sugar
2 small apples,
thinly sliced

In 3-quart casserole, place cider, allspice, cloves, nutmeg, cinnamon sticks, orange juice, lemon juice, sugar and apples. Microwave at HIGH (10) 12 to 18 minutes until hot. Strain before serving. Yield: 4 cups (127 calories per ½ cup serving).

Total Microwave Cooking Time 12 to 18 Minutes

PROTEIN 0.2 / FAT 0.3 / CARBOHYDRATE 32.1 / SODIUM 5 / CHOLESTEROL 0

Kentucky Mint Julep

1 cup sugar
½ cup water
1 cup fresh mint leaves
Bourbon
Mint sprigs

In 2-cup glass measure, combine sugar and water. Microwave at HIGH (10) 3 to 5 minutes or until hot and sugar is dissolved. Stir well. Add 1 cup mint leaves; let stand 2 hours. Strain into small glass jar; cover tightly and refrigerate.

For each julep: Pour 1 tablespoon mint syrup mixture over crushed ice in tall glass. Slowly add 2 ounces bourbon. Garnish with mint sprigs. Yield: 8 tablespoons syrup (228 calories per drink).

Total Microwave Cooking Time 3 to 5 Minutes

PROTEIN 0.0 / FAT 0.0 / CARBOHYDRATE 24.9 / SODIUM 1 / CHOLESTEROL 0

California Cocoa

¼ cup cocoa
¼ cup sugar
3 cups milk
2 teaspoons grated
    orange rind
¼ teaspoon almond
    extract
Cinnamon sticks

In 4-cup glass measure, combine cocoa and sugar. Add about ½ cup milk to make a smooth paste; stir in remaining milk, orange rind and almond extract, blending thoroughly. Microwave at HIGH (10) 4 to 7 minutes. Pour into mugs and add cinnamon sticks for stirring. Yield: 4 servings (175 calories each).

Total Microwave Cooking Time 4 to 7 Minutes

PROTEIN 6.9 / FAT 7.1 / CARBOHYDRATE 24.0 / SODIUM 90 / CHOLESTEROL 26

Zippy Tomato Cocktail

1 (12 oz.) can vegetable
    juice cocktail
½ cup beef broth
1 tablespoon lemon juice
1 teaspoon Worcestershire
    sauce
¼ teaspoon prepared
    horseradish
2 drops hot sauce
¼ cup vodka, optional
Celery sticks, optional

In 4-cup glass measure, combine vegetable juice cocktail, beef broth, lemon juice, Worcestershire sauce, horseradish and hot sauce. Microwave at HIGH (10) 5 to 7 minutes until hot; stir after 4 minutes. If desired, stir in vodka and serve with celery sticks. Yield: 2 cups (52 calories per cup).

Total Microwave Cooking Time 5 to 7 Minutes

PROTEIN 3.7 / FAT 0.1 / CARBOHYDRATE 10.3 / SODIUM 1048 / CHOLESTEROL 12

Irish Coffee

2 to 3 cups strong coffee
4 teaspoons sugar
6 oz. Irish whiskey
Sweetened whipped cream,
    optional

Pour ½ to ¾ cup coffee in each of 4 (10 to 12 oz.) cups. Microwave at HIGH (10) 1 to 2 minutes. For each drink, stir in 1 teaspoon sugar and 1½ ounces Irish whiskey; top with whipped cream, if desired. Yield: 4 cups (118 calories per cup).

Total Microwave Cooking Time 1 to 2 Minutes

PROTEIN 0.2 / FAT 0.0 / CARBOHYDRATE 4.9 / SODIUM 4 / CHOLESTEROL 0

Hot Buttered Rum

4 cups apple juice
4 cinnamon sticks
4 tablespoons brown sugar,
    packed
4 oz. rum
4 teaspoons butter
Dash nutmeg

In each of 4 (10 to 12 oz.) mugs, combine 1 cup apple juice, 1 cinnamon stick and 1 tablespoon sugar. Micro-wave at HIGH (10) 1 to 2 minutes. For each drink, stir in 1 oz. rum; top with 1 teaspoon butter and dash nutmeg. Yield: 4 cups (269 calories per cup).

Total Microwave Cooking Time 1 to 2 Minutes

PROTEIN 0.2 / FAT 4.2 / CARBOHYDRATE 42.4 / SODIUM 51 / CHOLESTEROL 10

Soups & Stews

Minestrone Soup

1½ lbs. stew beef, cut into
    ½-inch cubes, fat and
    gristle removed
5 cups hot water
1 medium onion, chopped
1 clove garlic, minced
1 teaspoon basil
¼ teaspoon pepper
1 (14½ oz.) can tomatoes
2 bay leaves
2 cups pasta, one-inch
    in length, uncooked
1½ cups zucchini, sliced
    ¼-inch thick
1 cup cabbage, finely
    shredded
1 (10 oz.) pkg. frozen
    green beans, thawed
½ cup celery, chopped
2 tablespoons fresh
    parsley, snipped
1 teaspoon salt
1 (10 oz.) pkg. frozen baby
    carrots, thawed
1 (16 oz.) can navy beans,
    drained

In 3-quart casserole, place beef, water, onion, garlic, basil, pepper, tomatoes and bay leaves. Cover. Microwave at HIGH (10) 20 to 25 minutes until meat is tender. Add pasta, zucchini, cabbage, green beans, celery, parsley and salt. Cover. Microwave at HIGH (10) 14 to 17 minutes until vegetables and pasta are tender. Add baby carrots and navy beans. Cover. Microwave at HIGH (10) 10 to 12 minutes; stir after 5 minutes. Remove bay leaves. Cover and let stand 5 minutes before serving. Yield: 10 servings (345 calories each).

Total Microwave Cooking Time 44 to 54 Minutes
Makes 8 to 10 servings

PROTEIN 20.3 / FAT 14.3 / CARBOHYDRATE 34.1 / SODIUM 578 / CHOLESTEROL 47

Cheese Soup with Broccoli, Cauliflower and Sausage

2 tablespoons butter
8 oz. smoked beef sausage
    or kielbasa, cubed
1 medium onion, chopped
½ teaspoon caraway seed,
    crushed
Dash pepper
1 bay leaf
2 (14½ oz.) cans chicken
    broth
3 medium potatoes, peeled
    and sliced
1½ cups broccoli flowerets
·1½ cups cauliflower
    flowerets
¼ cup whipping cream
1½ cups sharp Cheddar
    cheese, shredded

In 2-quart casserole, place butter, sausage, onion, caraway seed, pepper and bay leaf. Microwave at HIGH (10) 4 to 6 minutes until sausage begins to brown and onion is tender, stirring every 2 minutes. Add chicken broth, potatoes, broccoli and cauliflower. Microwave at MEDIUM HIGH (7) 28 to 32 minutes until vegetables are tender, stirring every 7 minutes. Stir in cream and Microwave at HIGH (10) 4 to 6 minutes until heated through. Remove bay leaf. Add cheese and stir until completely melted. Serve immediately. Yield: 4 servings (636 calories per serving).

Total Microwave Cooking Time 36 to 44 Minutes

PROTEIN 32.7 / FAT 43.0 / CARBOHYDRATE 31.0 / SODIUM 2280 / CHOLESTEROL 120

Soups & Stews

▲ *Beef Stew*

Beef Stew

3 slices bacon, diced
1 small onion, sliced
1½ cups water
1 (1¾ oz.) pkg. dry onion soup mix
1 teaspoon thyme
1 teaspoon salt
¾ teaspoon oregano
½ teaspoon pepper
2 lbs. boneless beef chuck, cut into ½-inch cubes
½ lb. small fresh mushrooms, sliced
1 large potato, peeled and cut into ½-inch cubes
1 cup celery, sliced ½-inch thick
3 tablespoons cornstarch
½ cup water
1 (10 oz.) pkg. frozen cut green beans, thawed
1 (10 oz.) pkg. frozen baby carrots, thawed

In 3-quart casserole, place bacon and onion. Cover. Microwave at HIGH (10) 7 to 9 minutes; stir after 3 minutes. Add 1½ cups water, onion soup mix, thyme, salt, oregano and pepper. Add meat; stir well. Cover. Microwave at MEDIUM HIGH (7) 30 minutes; stir after 15 minutes. Add mushrooms, potato and celery. Cover. Microwave at MEDIUM HIGH (7) 30 minutes until meat and vegetables are tender, stirring every 10 minutes.

In 2-cup measure, combine cornstarch with ½ cup water, stirring to blend well. Add cornstarch mixture, green beans and carrots to stew; stir until blended. Cover. Microwave at HIGH (10) 7 to 10 minutes; stir after 3 minutes. Yield: 8 servings (234 calories per serving).

Total Microwave Cooking Time 1 hour 14 Minutes to 1 hour 19 Minutes

PROTEIN 27.9 / FAT 6.0 / CARBOHYDRATE 16.5 / SODIUM 458 / CHOLESTEROL 47

Cheddar Broccoli Soup

2 lbs. broccoli, chopped
½ cup onion, chopped
¼ cup green pepper,
    chopped
2 tablespoons butter
2 tablespoons fresh
    parsley, chopped
1 bay leaf
1 teaspoon thyme
6 black peppercorns
¼ teaspoon salt
⅛ teaspoon nutmeg
2 (14½ oz.) cans chicken
    broth
¼ cup all-purpose flour
3 egg yolks, beaten
1 cup whipping cream
1 cup sharp Cheddar
    cheese, shredded

In 3-quart casserole, combine broccoli, onion, green pepper, butter, parsley, bay leaf, thyme, peppercorns, salt and nutmeg. Cover. Microwave at HIGH (10) 8 to 10 minutes until broccoli is tender; stir after 4 minutes. Remove bay leaf. Spoon mixture into blender. Add 1 can chicken broth. Blend for 1 minute on low speed.

Blend flour and remaining broth in 3-quart casserole. Stir well using a wire whisk. Add broccoli mixture; stir to blend. Microwave at HIGH (10) 10 to 12 minutes; stir after 5 minutes.

In 1-quart casserole, blend eggs and cream. Gradually add egg mixture to soup, stirring constantly. Add cheese. Microwave at HIGH (10) 4 minutes until cheese is completely melted, stirring after 2 minutes. Yield: 6 servings (363 calories each).

Total Microwave Cooking Time 22 to 26 Minutes

PROTEIN 15.3 / FAT 29.1 / CARBOHYDRATE 11.9 / SODIUM 1103 / CHOLESTEROL 195

Combine cooked vegetables and seasonings in a blender.

Burgundy Beef Stew

2 medium carrots, sliced
    ¼-inch thick
1 large onion, chopped
4 slices bacon, diced
3 cloves garlic, finely
    chopped
1½ cups red Burgundy
    wine
¼ cup brandy
2 teaspoons salt
1½ teaspoons thyme
1 teaspoon oregano
¾ teaspoon pepper
3 lbs. boneless beef chuck,
    cut into 1-inch cubes
1 (8 oz.) pkg. frozen small
    whole onions, thawed
½ lb. small fresh
    mushrooms, quartered
¼ cup water
¼ cup all-purpose flour

In 3-quart casserole, place carrots, onion, bacon and garlic. Cover. Microwave at HIGH (10) 5 to 7 minutes until bacon is cooked and vegetables are tender; stir after 3 minutes. Blend in wine, brandy, salt, thyme, oregano and pepper. Add meat; stir well. Microwave at MEDIUM (5) 29 to 31 minutes. Add onions and mushrooms. Microwave at MEDIUM (5) 15 to 20 minutes until meat and vegetables are tender, stirring every 5 minutes.

In 1-cup measure, blend water and flour to make a smooth paste. Stir into stew. Cover. Microwave at HIGH (10) 5 to 7 minutes; stir after 3 minutes. Serve over noodles, if desired. Yield: 10 servings (444 calories each).

Total Microwave Cooking Time 54 to 65 Minutes

PROTEIN 27.4 / FAT 28.7 / CARBOHYDRATE 8.8 / SODIUM 610 / CHOLESTEROL 96

Soups & Stews

Cheesy Vegetable Soup

3 small carrots, grated
1 large potato, shredded
1 small onion, finely
    chopped
1 stalk celery, finely
    chopped
1 cup water
1 cup chicken broth
½ cup half & half
1½ cups sharp Cheddar
    cheese, shredded
Dash salt
Dash white pepper

In 2-quart casserole, combine carrots, potato, onion, celery and water. Cover. Microwave at HIGH (10) 9 to 12 minutes until potatoes are tender; stir after 5 minutes. Blend in chicken broth and half & half. Cover. Microwave at MEDIUM HIGH (7) 5 to 8 minutes until heated through. Add cheese, salt and pepper. Microwave at HIGH (10) 1 to 2 minutes. Yield: 4 servings (289 calories each).

Total Microwave Cooking Time 16 to 20 Minutes

PROTEIN 15.7 / FAT 18.3 / CARBOHYDRATE 15.9 / SODIUM 761 / CHOLESTEROL 56

Creamy Mushroom Soup

Coarsely chop stems and add to broth for flavor.

2 lbs. fresh mushrooms
2 (13 ¾ oz.) cans chicken
    broth
1 (1¾ oz.) pkg. dry onion
    soup mix
3 tablespoons butter, sliced
3 tablespoons all-purpose
    flour
1 cup whipping cream
3 egg yolks
¼ cup sherry
Dash hot sauce
Dash pepper
Dash salt

Thinly slice mushroom caps and set aside. Coarsely chop stems and place in 4-cup glass measure. Add 1 can of chicken broth. Microwave at HIGH (10) 10 minutes until broth is brown. Strain broth into 3-quart casserole; discard mushroom pieces. Add onion soup mix, remaining chicken broth, mushroom caps and butter. Microwave at HIGH (10) 15 to 18 minutes; stir after 7 minutes. In 4-cup glass measure, combine flour, cream and egg yolks; whisk until smooth. Gradually add cream mixture, sherry, hot sauce, pepper and salt to hot soup, stirring constantly with a wire whisk. Microwave at HIGH (10) 7 to 9 minutes until slightly thickened, stirring every 4 minutes. Yield: 8 servings (263 calories each).

Total Microwave Cooking Time 32 to 37 Minutes

PROTEIN 9.2 / FAT 20.2 / CARBOHYDRATE 11.3 / SODIUM 1589 / CHOLESTEROL 135

Chicken Noodle Soup

Strain broth and discard mushroom pieces before adding the soup mix.

2 lbs. chicken pieces
1 onion, sliced
4 celery stalks, sliced
2 bay leaves
2 teaspoons peppercorns
2 teaspoons salt
6 cups hot water
3 carrots, shredded
1 cup egg noodles,
    uncooked

In 3-quart casserole, combine chicken, onion, celery, bay leaves, peppercorns, salt and water. Cover. Microwave at HIGH (10) 10 minutes. Stir. Continue to Microwave at MEDIUM (5) 30 to 37 minutes until chicken is tender. Remove chicken from broth and set aside to cool. Add carrots and noodles to broth. Remove chicken from bone, coarsely chop and add to broth. Cover. Microwave at MEDIUM HIGH (7) 7 to 8 minutes until noodles and carrots are tender. Remove bay leaves. Yield: 8 servings (278 calories each).

Total Microwave Cooking Time 47 to 55 Minutes

PROTEIN 22.3 / FAT 17.4 / CARBOHYDRATE 7.1 / SODIUM 688 / CHOLESTEROL 90

Chili

1 lb. lean ground beef
1 medium onion, chopped
½ cup green pepper, chopped
1 (15 ½ oz.) can kidney beans
1 (14 ½ oz.) can whole tomatoes, chopped
1 (6 oz.) can tomato paste
½ cup water
1 teaspoon garlic salt
1 teaspoon chili powder
1 teaspoon oregano
½ teaspoon cumin
½ teaspoon cayenne pepper
Dash hot sauce

In 2-quart casserole, combine ground beef, onion and green pepper. Cover. Microwave at HIGH (10) 4 to 6 minutes until meat is browned, stirring every 2 minutes. Drain. Add kidney beans, tomatoes, tomato paste, water, garlic salt, chili powder, oregano, cumin, cayenne pepper and hot sauce; stir to blend. Cover. Microwave at MEDIUM HIGH (7) 20 to 25 minutes, stirring every 7 minutes. Let stand, covered, for 5 minutes before serving. Yield: 6 servings (257 calories each).

Total Microwave Cooking Time 24 to 31 Minutes

PROTEIN 15.9 / FAT 12.5 / CARBOHYDRATE 21.3 / SODIUM 777 / CHOLESTEROL 43

French Onion Soup

¼ cup butter
4 medium onions, thinly sliced
3 cloves garlic, minced
2 (10½ oz.) cans beef broth
2 tablespoons dry sherry
½ teaspoon salt
¼ teaspoon pepper
4 to 5 slices French bread, optional
1 to 1½ cups Swiss cheese, shredded, optional

In 3-quart casserole, place butter, onions and garlic. Microwave at HIGH (10) 5 to 8 minutes until onions are tender. Add beef broth, sherry, salt and pepper; stir to blend. Microwave at HIGH (10) 10 to 12 minutes. Yield: 5 servings (172 calories each).

Serving Suggestion: Top individual servings of soup with one slice of French bread covered with Swiss cheese. Microwave at HIGH (10) 30 to 45 seconds until cheese is completely melted.

Total Microwave Cooking Time 15½ to 20¾ Minutes

PROTEIN 7.8 / FAT 9.4 / CARBOHYDRATE 13.6 / SODIUM 1339 / CHOLESTEROL 54

Add cheese for topping and microwave.

Clam Chowder

1 tablespoon bacon drippings
2 tablespoons onion, diced
1 small potato, peeled and cubed
½ cup water
½ teaspoon seasoned salt
Dash pepper
1 tablespoon all-purpose flour
1 cup milk, divided
1 (6 ½ oz.) can minced clams
1 tablespoon butter

In 2-quart casserole, combine bacon drippings and onion. Microwave at HIGH (10) 1 ½ to 3 minutes until onion is tender. Add potato, water, seasoned salt and pepper. Cover. Microwave at HIGH (10) 4 to 6 minutes until potato is tender; stir after 2 minutes. Add flour to ¼ cup milk; stir well to blend. Add flour mixture, remaining ¾ cup milk, clams and butter to potato and onions. Microwave at HIGH (10) 4 to 8 minutes, stirring every 2 minutes. Yield: 3 servings (182 calories each).

Total Microwave Cooking Time 9½ to 17 Minutes

PROTEIN 8.3 / FAT 11.5 / CARBOHYDRATE 11.2 / SODIUM 724 / CHOLESTEROL 41

Meats

Flank Steak Florentine

1½ to 1¾ lbs. beef flank
   steak
½ cup fresh mushrooms,
   chopped
1 medium onion, chopped
1 small carrot,
   finely chopped
1 clove garlic, minced
3 tablespoons butter
1 (10 oz.) pkg. frozen
   chopped spinach,
   thawed and well drained
2 teaspoons instant beef
   bouillon granules
¼ cup hot water
1 (10¾ oz.) can cream of
   chicken soup
2 tablespoons capers,
   drained
2 tablespoons dry
   vermouth, optional
½ teaspoon curry powder
¼ teaspoon coriander
¼ teaspoon white pepper

Pound flank steak with a mallet to ⅛-inch thickness; score with a sharp knife. In 1½-quart casserole, combine mushrooms, onion, carrot, garlic, butter and spinach. Cover. Microwave at HIGH (10) 1 to 4 minutes. Spread spinach mixture over steak. Starting at long side, roll steak in jelly roll fashion. Tie with string or secure with toothpicks.

Place steak, seam side up, in 2-quart oblong glass baking dish. In 4-cup glass measure, dissolve bouillon granules in hot water. Add soup, capers, vermouth, curry powder, coriander and pepper. Pour over steak; cover with vented plastic wrap. Microwave at HIGH (10) 8 to 10 minutes. Microwave at LOW (3) 32 to 42 minutes; turn steak over after 20 minutes and baste with sauce. Let stand, covered, 10 minutes before serving. Yield: 4 servings (494 calories per serving).

Total Microwave Cooking Time 43 to 56 Minutes

PROTEIN 22.0 / FAT 31.5 / CARBOHYDRATE 13.5 / SODIUM 1250 / CHOLESTEROL 118

Marinated Pot Roast

1 (3 to 4 lb.) boneless
   chuck roast
1 teaspoon pepper
½ teaspoon salt
¼ teaspoon garlic powder
¾ cup zesty Italian salad
   dressing
1 (10 oz.) pkg. frozen
   baby carrots, thawed
½ lb. sliced fresh
   mushrooms
1 (6 oz.) can tomato paste

Pierce roast on both sides with a fork. Place in 2-quart oblong glass baking dish. Combine pepper, salt and garlic powder; sprinkle over roast. Pour salad dressing over roast. Cover and refrigerate 6 to 8 hours, turning twice.

Cover with vented plastic wrap. Microwave at HIGH (10) 12 to 15 minutes. Microwave at MEDIUM (5) 42 to 58 minutes; turn roast over after 25 minutes. Add carrots and mushrooms. Cover and Microwave at MEDIUM (5) 7 to 11 minutes until meat and vegetables are tender. Remove meat and vegetables to warm platter. Add tomato paste to cooking liquid; stir well. Microwave at HIGH (10) 2 to 4 minutes. Serve with meat and vegetables. Yield: 6 servings (781 calories per serving).

Total Microwave Cooking Time 1 Hour 23 Minutes
to 1 Hour 28 Minutes

PROTEIN 44.1 / FAT 60.7 / CARBOHYDRATE 13.4 / SODIUM 924 / CHOLESTEROL 156

Meats

▲ *Stuffed Peppers*

Stuffed Peppers

**6 medium yellow,
    green or red peppers**
1½ lbs. lean ground beef
**1 cup cooked long grain
    rice**
½ cup onion, chopped
½ cup celery, diced
**1 small tomato, seeded
    and chopped**
1 clove garlic, minced
1 teaspoon salt
¼ teaspoon pepper
**1 (10¾ oz.) can condensed
    tomato soup**
½ teaspoon basil
**½ cup sharp Cheddar
    cheese, shredded**

Cut off tops of peppers. Remove seeds and membrane. In large bowl, combine beef, rice, onion, celery, tomato, garlic, salt and pepper. Fill peppers with meat mixture. Arrange in 2-quart oblong glass baking dish. Combine soup and basil; pour over peppers. Cover. Microwave at HIGH (10) 20 to 24 minutes.

Sprinkle cheese over peppers. Let stand, covered, 5 minutes to melt cheese. Yield: 6 servings (444 calories per serving).

Total Microwave Cooking Time 20 to 24 Minutes

PROTEIN 25.1 / FAT 27.9 / CARBOHYDRATE 22.5 / SODIUM 1023 / CHOLESTEROL 95

Savory Swiss Steak

**1½ lbs. boneless round
    steak, pounded
    ¼-inch thick**
**1 (14½ oz.) can whole
    tomatoes, chopped**
1 (8 oz.) can tomato sauce
**1 (1¾ oz.) pkg. dry onion-
    mushroom soup mix**
**2 tablespoons fresh
    parsley, snipped**
1 teaspoon basil
¼ teaspoon oregano

Cut steak into serving size portions. In 2-quart casserole, combine steak, tomatoes, tomato sauce, soup mix, parsley, basil and oregano. Cover. Microwave at HIGH (10) 4 to 5 minutes and at MEDIUM (5) 35 to 40 minutes. Let stand, covered, 5 minutes before serving. Yield: 6 servings (318 calories per serving).

Total Microwave Cooking Time 39 to 45 Minutes

PROTEIN 24.4 / FAT 20.6 / CARBOHYDRATE 8.3 / SODIUM 1509 / CHOLESTEROL 75

Cheese-Stuffed Meat Loaf

1½ cups soft
    bread crumbs
1 egg, slightly beaten
1½ teaspoons seasoned
    salt
¼ teaspoon pepper
½ cup milk
¾ cup onion, chopped,
    divided
1½ lbs. lean ground beef
2 tablespoons green
    pepper, chopped
2 tablespoons celery,
    chopped
1 (2 oz.) jar sliced
    pimento, drained
1 tablespoon lemon juice
1 egg, slightly beaten
1 cup Cheddar cheese,
    shredded
½ cup soft bread crumbs

In large mixing bowl, combine 1½ cups bread crumbs, 1 egg, seasoned salt, pepper, milk, ½ cup chopped onion and ground beef.

In 1½-quart casserole, combine ¼ cup chopped onion, green pepper, celery, pimento and lemon juice. Microwave at HIGH (10) 2 to 3 minutes until crisp-tender. Add egg; blend well. Stir in cheese and ½ cup bread crumbs.

On strip of wax paper, shape meat mixture into 14x7-inch rectangle. Spread cheese mixture over meat. Lifting wax paper for support, roll meat mixture from short side in jelly roll fashion. Place seam-side down in 9x5-inch glass loaf dish. Cover with vented plastic wrap. Microwave at MEDIUM HIGH (7) 25 to 28 minutes. Add topping (see below) and Microwave, uncovered, at MEDIUM HIGH (7) 4 to 5 minutes. Let stand 5 minutes. Yield: 6 servings (471 calories per serving).

Spicy Tomato Topping: In small bowl, combine ¾ cup catsup, ¼ cup brown sugar, ¾ teaspoon dry mustard, ¼ teaspoon allspice and ⅛ teaspoon cloves.

Total Microwave Cooking Time 29 to 36 Minutes

PROTEIN 29.6 / FAT 32.9 / CARBOHYDRATE 11.9 / SODIUM 751 / CHOLESTEROL 194

Spread cheese mixture over meat within ½-inch from sides.

Carefully roll up meat mixture from the short side to form roll.

Oriental Beef and Vegetables

1 lb. boneless top sirloin
    steak
1 clove garlic, minced
2 tablespoons soy sauce
2 tablespoons dry sherry
2 tablespoons water
1 tablespoon cornstarch
1 teaspoon brown sugar
¼ teaspoon ginger
⅛ teaspoon dry mustard
2 teaspoons oil
1 (6 oz.) pkg. frozen pea
    pods, thawed
1 medium sweet red
    pepper, cut into strips
1 (8 oz.) can sliced water
    chestnuts, drained

Slice steak diagonally across grain into 2½ x ½-inch strips. In medium bowl, combine garlic, soy sauce, sherry, water, cornstarch, brown sugar, ginger and mustard. Add beef, mix well and refrigerate 30 minutes. Drain, reserving marinade.

Place beef and oil in 2-quart oblong glass baking dish. Cover with wax paper. Microwave at HIGH (10) 8 to 10 minutes until beef is no longer pink; stir after 5 minutes. Add reserved marinade, pea pods, red pepper and water chestnuts. Cover. Microwave at HIGH (10) 7 to 9 minutes until sauce is thickened and vegetables are crisp-tender; stir after 4 minutes. Yield: 4 servings (389 calories per serving).

Total Microwave Cooking Time 15 to 19 Minutes

PROTEIN 22.9 / FAT 25.4 / CARBOHYDRATE 14.5 / SODIUM 481 / CHOLESTEROL 78

Tuck wax paper under ends of dish to hold securely in place.

Meats

Easy Beef and Biscuits

1 (9 oz.) pkg. frozen
   French-cut green beans
¼ cup onion, chopped
2 cups chopped,
   cooked beef
1 cup beef broth
¼ cup water
1½ tablespoons cornstarch
1 (4 oz.) can sliced
   mushrooms, drained
1¾ cups all-purpose flour
2½ teaspoons
   baking powder
½ teaspoon salt
⅓ cup shortening
1 cup milk
Chopped parsley
Paprika

In 2-quart casserole, place beans and onion; cover. Microwave at HIGH (10) 4 minutes, stirring after 2 minutes. Stir in beef and broth. Combine water and cornstarch; add to meat mixture. Cover and Microwave at HIGH (10) 4 minutes; add mushrooms. Microwave at HIGH (10) 4 to 7 minutes until hot and bubbly, stirring after 3 minutes.

Combine flour, baking powder and salt. Cut shortening into flour mixture with pastry blender until mixture resembles fine crumbs. Stir in milk until soft dough forms. Drop dough by 12 tablespoonfuls around edge of dish. Sprinkle biscuits with parsley and paprika. Microwave, uncovered, at HIGH (10) 4 to 7 minutes until biscuits appear done. Rotate dish ½ turn after 3 minutes. Cover loosely with plastic wrap and let stand 5 minutes. Yield: 6 servings (426 calories per serving).

Total Microwave Cooking Time 16 to 22 Minutes

PROTEIN 25.1 / FAT 19.9 / CARBOHYDRATE 35.8 / SODIUM 507 / CHOLESTEROL 64

Taco Salad

1½ lbs. lean ground beef
½ cup onion, chopped
1 cup green pepper,
   chopped
1 (16 oz.) can hot chili
   beans in chili gravy
1 (10 oz.) can mild
   enchilada sauce
1 (8 oz.) can tomato sauce
1 (8 oz.) can mild taco
   sauce
1 (10 oz.) pkg. corn chips
1 cup Cheddar cheese,
   shredded
4 cups lettuce, shredded
2 cups tomatoes, chopped

In 1½-quart casserole, crumble beef. Add onion and green pepper; cover. Microwave at HIGH (10) 6 to 8 minutes; stir after 3 minutes. Drain well. Add chili beans. Cover. Microwave at HIGH (10) 5 to 8 minutes until hot. Set aside and keep warm.

In 2-quart casserole, combine enchilada sauce, tomato sauce and taco sauce. Microwave at HIGH (10) 6 to 9 minutes; stir after 2 minutes.

In large salad bowl, layer corn chips, meat mixture, half of cheese, lettuce and tomatoes. Top with sauce and sprinkle with remaining cheese. Serve immediately. Yield: 8 servings (512 calories per serving).

Total Microwave Cooking Time 14 to 20 Minutes

PROTEIN 22.0 / FAT 31.3 / CARBOHYDRATE 36.4 / SODIUM 1098 / CHOLESTEROL 63

Scandinavian Meatballs

1 lb. lean ground beef
1 cup soft bread crumbs
¼ cup milk
1 egg
½ teaspoon salt
¼ teaspoon pepper
¼ teaspoon nutmeg
⅛ teaspoon allspice
½ teaspoon instant beef
   bouillon granules
½ cup hot water
1½ tablespoons
   all-purpose flour
½ cup half & half

Combine ground beef, bread crumbs, milk, egg, salt, pepper, nutmeg and allspice. Shape into 12 meatballs. Place meatballs in 2-quart oblong glass baking dish. Cover with wax paper. Microwave at HIGH (10) 5 to 8 minutes, rearranging meatballs after 3 minutes. Remove meatballs to warm platter. Reserve 2 tablespoons drippings and return to dish.

Dissolve bouillon granules in hot water. Add flour to reserved drippings; stir until smooth. Gradually stir in bouillon and half & half. Microwave at HIGH (10) 3 to 5 minutes until thickened, stirring every 2 minutes. Return meatballs to dish; turn to coat evenly. Microwave at HIGH (10) 3 to 4 minutes until hot. Serve over noodles. Yield: 4 servings (414 calories per serving).

For evenly shaped meatballs, use an ice cream scoop to divide meat mixture.

Total Microwave Cooking Time 11 to 17 Minutes

PROTEIN 24.7 / FAT 29.4 / CARBOHYDRATE 10.4 / SODIUM 478 / CHOLESTEROL 163

Pepper Steak

4 (6 oz.) cube steaks
⅓ cup steak sauce
1 (10 oz.) can
   beef consomme
½ teaspoon salt
¼ teaspoon pepper
¼ cup water
2 tablespoons cornstarch
1 medium green pepper,
   cut into strips
2 medium tomatoes,
   cut into chunks

In 2-quart casserole, place cube steaks, overlapping if necessary. Brush with steak sauce; cover. Microwave at MEDIUM HIGH (7) 8 to 10 minutes. Add consomme, salt and pepper; cover. Microwave at MEDIUM (5) 16 to 20 minutes. Remove steaks from sauce and keep warm.

Combine water and cornstarch; add to sauce. Microwave at HIGH (10) 1 to 3 minutes until thickened; stir once. Return meat to sauce; add green pepper and tomatoes. Microwave at MEDIUM (5) 3 to 6 minutes until hot. Yield: 4 servings (417 calories per serving).

Total Microwave Cooking Time 28 to 39 Minutes

PROTEIN 37.8 / FAT 21.7 / CARBOHYDRATE 13.0 / SODIUM 1046 / CHOLESTEROL 116

German-Style Pork Chops and Sauerkraut

4 (8 oz.) rib pork chops,
   1-inch thick
½ cup onion, chopped
1 (15 oz.) can sauerkraut,
   rinsed and drained
1 teaspoon caraway seeds
1 cup beer

In 8-inch square glass baking dish, arrange chops with thickest meaty areas to outside edges. Sprinkle evenly with onion. Spread sauerkraut over onion. Sprinkle with caraway seeds. Pour beer over meat and sauerkraut mixture; cover with vented plastic wrap. Microwave at MEDIUM (5) 28 to 40 minutes. Yield: 4 servings (767 calories per serving).

Total Microwave Cooking Time 28 to 40 Minutes

PROTEIN 42.3 / FAT 53.6 / CARBOHYDRATE 8.5 / SODIUM 792 / CHOLESTEROL 146

Meats

▲ *Apple-Stuffed Pork Chops*

Apple-Stuffed Pork Chops

To form a pocket, use a sharp knife to cut pork chop through center.

Place the stuffing in pocket.

**1 cup herb-seasoned
  stuffing mix**
⅔ cup apple, diced
**¼ cup onion,
  finely chopped**
3 tablespoons raisins
⅛ cup orange juice
**2 tablespoons butter,
  melted**
**1 tablespoon grated
  orange rind**
½ teaspoon salt
¼ teaspoon cinnamon
¼ teaspoon allspice
⅛ teaspoon pepper
**4 (8 oz.) center-cut
  pork chops, 1-inch thick**
½ cup currant jelly
2 tablespoons orange juice

In mixing bowl, combine stuffing mix, apple, onion, raisins, ⅛ cup orange juice, butter, orange rind, salt, cinnamon, allspice and pepper. Cut a pocket in each pork chop. Divide stuffing evenly among chops.

Arrange chops in 2-quart oblong glass baking dish with thickest meaty areas to outside edges. In 1-cup glass measure, combine currant jelly and 2 tablespoons orange juice. Microwave at HIGH (10) 1 to 2 minutes; stir well. Pour half of mixture over chops. Cover with wax paper. Microwave at MEDIUM (5) 30 to 40 minutes; carefully turn chops over after 15 minutes.

Spoon remaining jelly mixture over chops before serving. Yield: 4 servings (941 calories per serving).

Total Microwave Cooking Time 31 to 42 Minutes

PROTEIN 43.2 / FAT 63.6 / CARBOHYDRATE 49.5 / SODIUM 771 / CHOLESTEROL 171

Italian Sloppy Joes

1½ lbs. mild bulk
  Italian sausage
½ cup onion, chopped
½ cup green pepper,
  chopped
1 (2¼ oz.) can sliced ripe
  olives, drained
1 (28 oz.) can whole
  tomatoes, drained and
  chopped
½ teaspoon oregano
¼ teaspoon salt
¼ teaspoon pepper
⅛ teaspoon garlic powder
3 hamburger buns, split
  and toasted
½ cup mozzarella cheese,
  shredded

In 2-quart casserole, crumble sausage. Add onion and green pepper; cover. Microwave at HIGH (10) 8 to 10 minutes; stir after 4 minutes. Drain well. Add olives, tomatoes, oregano, salt, pepper and garlic powder. Microwave at HIGH (10) 3 to 6 minutes until hot.

Serve over hamburger buns. Sprinkle with mozzarella cheese. Yield: 6 servings (496 calories per serving).

Total Microwave Cooking Time 11 to 16 Minutes

PROTEIN 15.0 / FAT 39.4 / CARBOHYDRATE 20.6 / SODIUM 1059 / CHOLESTEROL 72

When microwaving sausage, use a microwave-safe colander inside the casserole dish to eliminate draining.

Lemon Pork Chops

4 (8 oz.) center-cut
  pork chops, ¾-inch thick
½ teaspoon salt
¼ teaspoon pepper
⅛ teaspoon thyme
½ cup chili sauce
1 tablespoon brown sugar
4 onion slices
4 lemon slices

Sprinkle chops with salt, pepper and thyme. Arrange chops in 2-quart casserole. Combine chili sauce and brown sugar; pour over chops. Place onion and lemon slice on each chop. Cover. Microwave at MEDIUM HIGH (7) 30 to 35 minutes until tender.
Yield: 4 servings (242 calories per serving).

Total Microwave Cooking Time 30 to 35 Minutes

PROTEIN 12.0 / FAT 13.6 / CARBOHYDRATE 19.4 / SODIUM 775 / CHOLESTEROL 36

Peachy Glazed Ham Slice

1 (8¾ oz.) can peach
  slices, drained
2 tablespoons honey
2 tablespoons lemon juice
¼ teaspoon allspice
1 teaspoon grated
  lemon rind
1 (3 lb.) fully cooked
  boneless ham slice

In a blender container, combine peach slices, honey, lemon juice and allspice. Cover and blend until smooth; stir in lemon rind.

Place ham in 2-quart oblong glass baking dish. Cover with wax paper. Microwave at HIGH (10) 6 to 7 minutes. Uncover, brush with glaze and continue Microwaving at HIGH (10) 2 to 3 minutes. Pour remaining glaze in 2-cup glass measure. Microwave at HIGH (10) 1 to 2 minutes or until heated through. Spoon glaze over ham. Yield: 6 servings (347 calories per serving).

Total Microwave Cooking Time 9 to 12 Minutes

PROTEIN 38.7 / FAT 15.3 / CARBOHYDRATE 12.0 / SODIUM 2554 / CHOLESTEROL 100

Meats

▲ *Veal Roll-Ups*

Tasty Veal Chops

**6 (6 oz.) veal loin chops,
¾ -inch thick**
¼ cup water
¼ cup dry sherry
2 tablespoons soy sauce
¼ teaspoon marjoram
¼ teaspoon pepper
½ cup water
2 tablespoons cornstarch
**1 (4 oz.) can sliced
mushrooms, drained**
**1 (8 oz.) can sliced water
chestnuts, drained**

Place chops in 3-quart casserole. Combine ¼ cup water, sherry, soy sauce, marjoram and pepper; pour over chops. Cover and let stand at room temperature 1 hour; turn once. Microwave at MEDIUM HIGH (7) 16 to 22 minutes until tender; turn over after 10 minutes. Remove chops to warm platter.

Combine ½ cup water and cornstarch; stir until smooth. Add to cooking liquid. Microwave at HIGH (10) 2 to 4 minutes until thickened, stirring every minute. Add mushrooms and water chestnuts. Microwave at HIGH (10) 2 to 3 minutes until hot. Spoon sauce over chops. Yield: 6 servings (321 calories per serving).

Total Microwave Cooking Time 20 to 29 Minutes

PROTEIN 33.0 / FAT 15.5 / CARBOHYDRATE 7.7 / SODIUM 481 / CHOLESTEROL 134

Veal Roll-Ups

6 (8 oz.) boneless veal
   cutlets, ½-inch thick
6 thin slices Swiss cheese
6 thin slices boiled ham
2 eggs
¼ cup butter, melted
½ cup dry bread crumbs
¼ cup all-purpose flour
1 teaspoon salt
½ teaspoon paprika
¼ teaspoon onion powder
¼ teaspoon sage
¼ teaspoon pepper

Pound each cutlet with meat mallet to ¼-inch thickness. Place 1 slice cheese and 1 slice ham on each piece of veal. Roll up firmly and fasten with a toothpick.

In small bowl, beat together eggs and butter. In shallow dish, combine bread crumbs, flour, salt, paprika, onion powder, sage and pepper. Dip veal rolls in egg mixture, then roll in crumb mixture. Place rolls in 2-quart oblong glass baking dish. Cover with wax paper. Microwave at MEDIUM (5) 16 to 22 minutes. Yield: 6 servings (422 calories per serving).

Total Microwave Cooking Time 16 to 22 Minutes

PROTEIN 52.1 / FAT 17.6 / CARBOHYDRATE 10.8 / SODIUM 845 / CHOLESTEROL 224

Place cheese and ham on top of flattened veal cutlet.

Veal with Rosemary

1½ lbs. veal round steak,
   cut into strips
¼ cup butter
1 (4½ oz.) jar sliced
   mushrooms, drained
2 green onions, sliced
1½ teaspoons rosemary
½ teaspoon salt
¼ teaspoon pepper
1 tablespoon cornstarch
¼ cup water
2 tomatoes, cut in wedges
2 tablespoons fresh
   parsley, snipped

Place veal, butter, mushrooms, onions, rosemary, salt and pepper in 2-quart casserole; cover. Microwave at MEDIUM HIGH (7) 16 to 20 minutes. Combine cornstarch and water; stir until smooth. Add to veal mixture. Microwave at HIGH (10) 2 to 4 minutes until thickened; stir after 1 minute. Add tomatoes and parsley and Microwave at HIGH (10) 1 to 2 minutes until hot. Serve over noodles or rice. Yield: 6 servings (207 calories per serving).

Total Microwave Cooking Time 19 to 26 Minutes

PROTEIN 23.5 / FAT 10.7 / CARBOHYDRATE 3.1 / SODIUM 424 / CHOLESTEROL 110

Dip veal roll in egg mixture then roll in crumb mixture.

Veal Parmigiana

1 cup buttery
   cracker crumbs
½ teaspoon salt
¼ teaspoon pepper
¾ cup grated Parmesan
   cheese, divided
6 (8 oz.) veal cutlets
1 egg, beaten
1 cup mozzarella cheese,
   grated
2 (8 oz.) cans tomato sauce
1 teaspoon oregano

Combine crumbs, salt, pepper and ½ cup Parmesan cheese. Dip cutlets in beaten egg; coat both sides with crumb mixture. Place cutlets in 2-quart oblong glass baking dish; cover. Microwave at MEDIUM HIGH (7) 8 to 10 minutes. Turn cutlets over; sprinkle with mozzarella cheese. Combine tomato sauce and oregano; pour over cutlets. Sprinkle with ¼ cup Parmesan cheese; cover. Microwave at MEDIUM HIGH (7) 12 to 18 minutes until tender. Let stand, covered, 10 minutes. Yield: 6 servings (508 calories per serving).

Total Microwave Cooking Time 20 to 28 Minutes

PROTEIN 55.9 / FAT 21.4 / CARBOHYDRATE 19.9 / SODIUM 1330 / CHOLESTEROL 254

Meats

Zesty Lamb Kabobs

Self sealing bags may be used for marinating meats and vegetables, but are not recommended for microwaving.

1⅓ cups dry red wine
2 tablespoons oil
1 cup onions,
    finely chopped
2 cloves garlic, crushed
2 tablespoons
    Dijon mustard
1 bay leaf
¾ teaspoon salt
½ teaspoon pepper
½ teaspoon thyme
¼ teaspoon ginger
2 lbs. lamb,
    cut in 1-inch cubes
2 large green peppers,
    cut in 1-inch squares
2 large red peppers,
    cut in 1-inch squares
3 medium onions,
    cut in eighths

In 2-quart casserole, combine wine, oil, onion, garlic, mustard, bay leaf, salt, pepper, thyme and ginger. Add lamb cubes. Cover and marinate in refrigerator several hours or overnight. Remove lamb from marinade. Discard marinade.

On 8-inch wooden skewers, thread red or green pepper square, onion chunk and lamb cube. Repeat, ending with onion chunk and pepper square. Place 4 kabobs on microwave-safe plate. Microwave at HIGH (10) 7 to 9 minutes. Repeat with remaining kabobs. Serve on cooked rice, if desired. Yield: 4 servings (371 calories per serving).

Total Microwave Cooking Time 14 to 18 Minutes

PROTEIN 37.0 / FAT 13.3 / CARBOHYDRATE 18.7 / SODIUM 429 / CHOLESTEROL 111

Leg of Lamb with Mustard Glaze

½ cup Dijon mustard
1 teaspoon basil
¼ teaspoon thyme
¼ teaspoon white pepper
2 tablespoons vegetable oil
2 tablespoons
    Worcestershire sauce
1 (4 to 5 lb.) leg of lamb

Combine mustard, basil, thyme, pepper, oil and Worcestershire sauce. Pierce lamb in several places with fork. Spread mustard mixture over lamb. Place in cooking bag and chill 2 hours. Place fat side up on trivet in 2-quart oblong glass baking dish. Cook to desired doneness according to chart on page 35. Yield: 10 servings (334 calories per serving).

PROTEIN 24.4 / FAT 25.0 / CARBOHYDRATE 0.7 / SODIUM 269 / CHOLESTEROL 94

Mandarin Lamb Chops

4 (6 oz.) loin lamb chops,
    1-inch thick
1 (11 oz.) can Mandarin
    oranges
½ cup chutney, chopped
¼ cup sugar
2 tablespoons lemon juice
1 tablespoon cornstarch

In 8-inch square glass baking dish arrange chops with thickest meaty areas to outside edges. Cover with wax paper. Microwave at MEDIUM HIGH (7) 10 minutes; drain. Turn chops over. Drain oranges, reserving syrup. Combine ⅛ cup reserved syrup, chutney, sugar and lemon juice. Spoon mixture over chops; cover. Microwave at MEDIUM HIGH (7) 8 to 12 minutes until tender. Remove chops to serving platter and keep warm.

Combine cornstarch and remaining syrup. Add to juices in dish. Microwave at MEDIUM HIGH (7) 1 to 3 minutes until thickened, stirring once. Spoon sauce over chops. Yield: 4 servings (229 calories per serving).

Total Microwave Cooking Time 19 to 25 Minutes

PROTEIN 9.8 / FAT 2.6 / CARBOHYDRATE 43.3 / SODIUM 103 / CHOLESTEROL 28

TO INSERT PROBE: Measure the distance to the center of the roast by laying the temperature probe on top of the meat. Mark with your thumb and forefinger where the edge of the meat comes on the probe.

Insert probe horizontally up to the point marked by your finger. Make sure that tip of probe reaches the center of the meat. NOTE: For best results, place roast in cooking bag following manufacturers instructions.

Meat Roasting Chart for Microwave Cooking

MEAT*		Power Level	Approximate Cooking Time	Temperature Probe Setting
Beef	**Rib, Boneless Rib, Top Sirloin**			
	Rare	Medium (5)	11 to 14 min./lb.	140°F.
	Medium	Medium (5)	14 to 17 min./lb.	160°F.
	Well	Medium (5)	17 to 20 min./lb.	170°F.
	Standing Rib, high quality, bone-in roast			
	Rare	Medium (5)	11 to 14 min./lb.	140°F.
	Medium	Medium (5)	14 to 17 min./lb.	160°F.
	Well	Medium (5)	17 to 20 min./lb.	170°F.
	Pot Roast* (2½ to 3½ lb.)			
	Chuck	Medium (5)	22 to 29 min./lb.	
	Oblong glass baking dish with vented plastic wrap.			
	Rump	Medium (5)	22 to 29 min./lb.	
	3-quart casserole with lid.			
Pork	**Bone-in**	Medium (5)	13 to 18 min./lb.	170°F.
	Boneless	Medium (5)	13 to 18 min./lb.	170°F.
	Pork Chops* (½ to 1-inch thick)			
	2 chops	Medium High (7)	9 to 14 min. total	
	4 chops	Medium High (7)	14 to 17 min. total	
	6 chops	Medium High (7)	15 to 17 min. total	
Ham	**Canned (3 lb.)**	Medium (5)	10 to 14 min./lb.	140°F.
	Butt (3 to 4 lb.)	Medium (5)	14 to 18 min./lb.	140°F.
	Shank (3 to 4 lb.)	Medium (5)	14 to 18 min./lb.	140°F.
Lamb	**Bone-in**			
	Medium	Medium (5)	10 to 15 min./lb.	160°F.
	Well	Medium (5)	12 to 17 min./lb.	170°F.
	Boneless			
	Medium	Medium (5)	11 to 17 min./lb.	160°F.
	Well	Medium (5)	13 to 18 min./lb.	170°F.
	Lamb Chops* (½ to 1-inch thick)			
	2 chops	Medium High (7)	3 to 6 min. total	
	4 chops	Medium High (7)	6 to 9 min. total	
	8 chops	Medium High (7)	9 to 11 min. total	

*Turn over after half of cooking time.

Poultry

Oriental Chicken and Cashews

3 tablespoons oil
4 (6 oz.) boneless chicken
    breast halves, skinned
    & thinly sliced
2 cloves garlic, minced
2 tablespoons soy sauce
1 tablespoon sherry
1 tablespoon cornstarch
¼ teaspoon ginger
1 medium green pepper,
    cut into small chunks
½ cup cashews

Place oil in 2-quart oblong glass baking dish. Microwave at HIGH (10) 1 minute. Combine chicken, garlic, soy sauce, sherry, cornstarch and ginger; add to oil. Microwave at HIGH (10) 3 to 4 minutes, stirring every minute. Add green pepper and cashews. Cover with plastic wrap. Microwave at HIGH (10) 3 to 5 minutes until chicken is done and green pepper is crisp-tender; stir after 1 minute. Let stand 3 minutes before serving. Serve over rice. Yield: 4 servings (397 calories per serving).

Total Microwave Cooking Time 7 to 10 Minutes

PROTEIN 42.5 / FAT 20.4 / CARBOHYDRATE 9.4 / SODIUM 636 / CHOLESTEROL 99

Sweet and Tangy Chicken

1 (2 ½ to 3 ½ lb.) chicken,
    cut up
¼ cup mayonnaise
1 (1¾ oz.) pkg. dry onion
    soup mix
1 cup bottled Russian
    dressing
1 cup apricot-pineapple
    preserves

Arrange chicken in 2-quart oblong glass baking dish with thickest meaty pieces to outside edges. In small mixing bowl, combine mayonnaise, onion soup mix, dressing and preserves. Pour over chicken. Cover with vented plastic wrap. Microwave at HIGH (10) 18 to 26 minutes until chicken is thoroughly cooked.
Yield: 6 servings (848 calories per serving).

Total Microwave Cooking Time 18 to 26 Minutes

PROTEIN 37.0 / FAT 58.4 / CARBOHYDRATE 44.3 / SODIUM 1717 / CHOLESTEROL 147

Spicy Marinated Chicken

2 cloves garlic, crushed
3 tablespoons lemon juice
½ teaspoon cinnamon
½ teaspoon ginger
½ teaspoon nutmeg
½ teaspoon coriander
½ teaspoon paprika
¼ teaspoon turmeric
⅛ teaspoon cayenne
    pepper
2 (12 oz.) whole boneless
    chicken breasts, split
    and skinned
½ cup sour cream

In small bowl, combine garlic, lemon juice, cinnamon, ginger, nutmeg, coriander, paprika, turmeric and cayenne pepper. Place chicken breasts in 8-inch square glass baking dish. Brush spice mixture over chicken. Cover with plastic wrap and refrigerate several hours or overnight. Remove dish from refrigerator; vent plastic wrap. Microwave at HIGH (10) 12 to 17 minutes; turn over after 7 minutes. Top with sour cream. Yield: 4 servings (257 calories per serving).

Total Microwave Cooking Time 12 to 17 Minutes

PROTEIN 40.4 / FAT 8.4 / CARBOHYDRATE 3.0 / SODIUM 129 / CHOLESTEROL 111

Poultry

▲ *Chicken Cacciatore*

Chicken Cacciatore

**1 (2½ to 3 lb.) chicken,
  cut up**
**1 medium green pepper,
  coarsely chopped**
1 medium onion, sliced
**1 large tomato, seeded and
  coarsely chopped**
1 (15 oz.) can tomato sauce
1 (6 oz.) can tomato paste
¼ cup dry white wine
1 bay leaf
2 cloves garlic, minced
½ teaspoon oregano
½ teaspoon salt
¼ teaspoon fennel seed
¼ teaspoon pepper
**½ cup grated
  Parmesan cheese**
**Capellini or spaghetti
  (optional)**

In 3-quart casserole, place chicken pieces with meaty portions along outside of dish. Add green pepper and onion slices.

In 4-cup glass measure, combine tomato, tomato sauce, tomato paste, wine, bay leaf, garlic, oregano, salt, fennel seed and pepper. Mix well and pour over chicken. Cover. Microwave at HIGH (10) 27 to 32 minutes until chicken is done and vegetables are tender; rearrange chicken pieces after 10 minutes. Remove bay leaf. Sprinkle with Parmesan cheese. Serve over capellini or spaghetti. Yield: 6 servings (511 calories per serving).

Total Microwave Cooking Time 27 to 32 Minutes

PROTEIN 40.7 / FAT 31.1 / CARBOHYDRATE 15.8 / SODIUM 905 / CHOLESTEROL 147

Hot Chicken Salad

1 ½ cups cooked chicken, diced
½ cup celery, finely chopped
½ cup slivered almonds, toasted
½ cup buttery cracker crumbs
¼ cup onion, chopped
1 (10 ¾ oz.) can cream of chicken soup
½ cup mayonnaise
½ teaspoon salt
¾ cup Cheddar cheese, shredded

In 1 ½-quart casserole, combine chicken, celery, almonds, cracker crumbs, onion, chicken soup, mayonnaise and salt. Mix well. Cover. Microwave at HIGH (10) 9 to 11 minutes. Sprinkle cheese over top. Microwave at HIGH (10) 1 to 3 minutes until cheese melts. Yield: 4 servings (633 calories per serving).

Total Microwave Cooking Time 10 to 14 Minutes

PROTEIN 27.0 / FAT 51.5 / CARBOHYDRATE 17.2 / SODIUM 1486 / CHOLESTEROL 91

Chicken Parmesan

¾ cup seasoned dry bread crumbs
¼ cup grated Parmesan cheese
¼ teaspoon paprika
1 egg, beaten
¼ cup water
4 (6 oz.) boneless chicken breasts, skinned, split and pounded thin
1 cup spaghetti sauce
1 cup mozzarella cheese, shredded

In small mixing bowl, combine bread crumbs, Parmesan cheese and paprika. Set aside. In shallow dish, blend egg and water together. Dip chicken breasts in egg mixture and then in bread crumb mixture. In 2-quart oblong glass baking dish, arrange chicken. Pour spaghetti sauce over top and sprinkle with mozzarella cheese. Cover with wax paper. Microwave at HIGH (10) 13 to 18 minutes. Yield: 4 servings (417 calories per serving).

Total Microwave Cooking Time 13 to 18 Minutes

PROTEIN 52.1 / FAT 13.4 / CARBOHYDRATE 19.5 / SODIUM 742 / CHOLESTEROL 190

Pound chicken breast to ¼-inch thickness.

Savory Chicken Bites

1 ½ cups dry bread crumbs
½ cup grated Parmesan cheese
1 tablespoon thyme
1 tablespoon basil
1 teaspoon salt
½ teaspoon lemon pepper
¾ cup butter, melted
½ teaspoon hot sauce
8 (6 oz.) boneless chicken breast halves, skinned and cubed

In shallow dish, combine bread crumbs, Parmesan cheese, thyme, basil, salt and lemon pepper. Mix well. In small mixing bowl, combine butter and hot sauce. Dip chicken pieces in butter and coat with bread crumb mixture. Place coated chicken pieces in single layer in 2-quart oblong glass baking dish. Microwave at HIGH (10) 9 to 12 minutes until thoroughly cooked. Yield: 8 servings (439 calories per serving).

Total Microwave Cooking Time 9 to 12 Minutes

PROTEIN 44.0 / FAT 21.8 / CARBOHYDRATE 14.7 / SODIUM 834 / CHOLESTEROL 150

Poultry

▲ *Chicken with Spicy Cheddar Sauce*

Chicken with Spicy Cheddar Sauce

½ cup cornflake crumbs
½ teaspoon paprika
¼ teaspoon garlic powder
4 (6 oz.) boneless chicken
  breast halves, skinned
½ cup cheese spread with
  jalapeño peppers
¼ cup ripe olives, sliced
1 (2 oz.) jar sliced pimento,
  drained

In medium mixing bowl, combine cornflake crumbs, paprika and garlic powder. Rinse chicken in water, then coat with crumb mixture. In 2-quart oblong glass baking dish, arrange chicken with meaty portions toward the edges of the dish. Cover. Microwave at HIGH (10) 13 to 17 minutes until thoroughly cooked. Transfer chicken to platter and keep warm.

In 2-cup glass measure, combine cheese spread, olives and pimento. Microwave at HIGH (10) 1 minute until heated through. Pour sauce over chicken.
Yield: 4 servings (386 calories per serving).

Total Microwave Cooking Time 14 to 18 Minutes

PROTEIN 48.5 / FAT 13.6 / CARBOHYDRATE 14.8 / SODIUM 985 / CHOLESTEROL 126

Moroccan Chicken

1 (2½ to 3½ lb.) chicken,
  cut up
1 cup onions, chopped
2 cups carrots, sliced
  ½-inch thick
¾ cup chicken broth
1 tablespoon lemon juice
2 teaspoons grated
  lemon rind
1 teaspoon paprika
½ teaspoon ginger
¼ teaspoon turmeric
⅛ teaspoon cinnamon
3 cups cooked rice,
  optional

In 3-quart casserole, place chicken pieces with meaty portions along outside of dish. Add onions and carrots. Combine broth, lemon juice, lemon rind, paprika, ginger, turmeric and cinnamon. Pour over chicken. Cover. Microwave at HIGH (10) 25 to 29 minutes until chicken is done and vegetables are tender. Serve over rice, if desired. Yield: 6 servings (460 calories per serving).

Total Microwave Cooking Time 25 to 29 Minutes

PROTEIN 37.7 / FAT 29.0 / CARBOHYDRATE 10.7 / SODIUM 356 / CHOLESTEROL 142

Chicken A La Roma

2 tablespoons olive oil
¾ cup green onions,
   thinly sliced
2 cloves garlic, minced
½ lb. sliced fresh
   mushrooms
1 (8 oz.) can tomato sauce
1 (6 oz.) can tomato paste
1 (2¼ oz.) can sliced ripe
   olives, drained
½ cup dry white wine
1 tablespoon instant
   chicken bouillon
   granules
2 teaspoons parsley flakes
1 teaspoon basil
1 teaspoon oregano
½ teaspoon thyme
¼ teaspoon pepper
1 (2½ to 3 lb.) chicken,
   cut up
1 (6 oz.) jar marinated
   artichoke hearts, drained
¼ cup grated
   Parmesan cheese

In 8-inch square glass baking dish, place oil, onion, garlic and mushrooms. Cover with wax paper. Microwave at HIGH (10) 4 to 6 minutes. Drain.

In 4-cup glass measure, combine tomato sauce, tomato paste, olives, white wine, bouillon, parsley, basil, oregano, thyme and pepper. Add onion, garlic and mushroom mixture.

Place chicken pieces in baking dish. Add tomato mixture. Cover. Microwave at HIGH (10) 18 to 21 minutes. Arrange artichoke hearts around chicken pieces and sprinkle with Parmesan cheese. Cover. Microwave at HIGH (10) 3 to 5 minutes. Let stand 5 minutes before serving. Yield: 6 servings (544 calories per serving).

Total Microwave Cooking Time 25 to 32 Minutes

PROTEIN 40.4 / FAT 35.9 / CARBOHYDRATE 15.9 / SODIUM 1140 / CHOLESTEROL 145

Chicken Italiano

2 tablespoons olive oil
½ lb. sliced fresh
   mushrooms
½ cup onion, chopped
2 cloves garlic, minced
6 (6 oz.) boneless chicken
   breast halves, skinned
⅔ cup dry white wine
¾ teaspoon Italian herb
   seasoning
¼ teaspoon basil
1 cup spaghetti sauce
¼ cup grated
   Parmesan cheese
¼ teaspoon red pepper
   flakes

In 3-quart casserole, place oil, mushrooms, onion and garlic. Microwave at HIGH (10) 2 to 4 minutes until tender. Add chicken. Combine wine, Italian seasoning, basil and spaghetti sauce. Pour over chicken. Microwave at MEDIUM HIGH (7) 14 to 16 minutes. Turn over after 8 minutes. Sprinkle with Parmesan cheese and red pepper flakes. Microwave at HIGH (10) 3 to 5 minutes. Yield: 6 servings (299 calories per serving).

Total Microwave Cooking Time 19 to 25 Minutes

PROTEIN 42.3 / FAT 8.7 / CARBOHYDRATE 7.4 / SODIUM 364 / CHOLESTEROL 101

To bone chicken breast, split the breast in half lengthwise.

Starting at the breast bone side of the chicken, slice meat away from the bone.

Poultry

Remove the center of pastry shells before filling.

Chicken In Pastry Shells

1 tablespoon butter
1 cup fresh mushrooms, sliced
½ cup green pepper, chopped
2 tablespoons butter, melted
3 tablespoons all-purpose flour
½ cup chicken broth
½ cup milk
2 tablespoons dry sherry
½ teaspoon salt
¼ teaspoon pepper
2 (5 oz.) cans cooked chicken, drained
6 pastry shells, baked

In 2-quart casserole, place 1 tablespoon butter, mushrooms and green pepper. Microwave at HIGH (10) 2 to 4 minutes until mushrooms are tender; stir after 2 minutes. Drain.

In 4-cup glass measure, combine remaining butter and flour. Gradually add broth and milk, stirring constantly until smooth. Microwave at HIGH (10) 2 to 4 minutes until thickened, stirring every minute. Add mushrooms, green pepper, sherry, salt, pepper and chicken. Microwave at HIGH (10) 4 to 7 minutes until heated through. Serve in baked pastry shells. Yield: 6 servings (396 calories per serving).

Total Microwave Cooking Time 8 to 15 Minutes

PROTEIN 19.1 / FAT 25.3 / CARBOHYDRATE 21.5 / SODIUM 617 / CHOLESTEROL 61

Chicken Gumbo

1 (2½ to 3 lb.) chicken, cut up
2 tablespoons oil
2 cups onion, chopped
1 small green pepper, chopped
1 small sweet red pepper, chopped
¼ cup all-purpose flour
2 (10¾ oz.) cans chicken broth
½ teaspoon salt
½ teaspoon pepper
1 lb. smoked sausage, cut into ¼-inch slices

In 3-quart casserole, place chicken and oil. Cover. Microwave at HIGH (10) 10 to 12 minutes; turn chicken over after 5 minutes. Combine onion, green pepper and red pepper; add to chicken. Microwave at HIGH (10) 6 to 7 minutes until tender.

Combine flour, chicken broth, salt and pepper; stir until blended. Pour over chicken and vegetables. Microwave at HIGH (10) 6 to 8 minutes until thickened. Add sausage. Microwave at HIGH (10) 3 to 5 minutes until heated. Yield: 8 servings (579 calories per serving).

Total Microwave Cooking Time 25 to 32 Minutes

PROTEIN 38.8 / FAT 42.0 / CARBOHYDRATE 9.2 / SODIUM 1221 / CHOLESTEROL 147

Curried Chicken and Rice

2 tablespoons butter
6 (6 oz.) boneless chicken breast halves, skinned and cut into ½-inch cubes
1 medium onion, chopped
2 (10¾ oz.) cans cream of chicken soup
¼ cup fresh parsley, snipped
2 teaspoons curry powder
¼ teaspoon seasoned salt
⅛ teaspoon pepper
3 cups cooked rice

In 3-quart casserole, place butter, chicken and onion. Microwave at HIGH (10) 6 to 8 minutes until chicken is no longer pink, stirring every 2 minutes. Add chicken soup, parsley, curry, seasoned salt, pepper and rice; stir. Cover and Microwave at HIGH (10) 6 to 8 minutes. Yield: 6 servings (457 calories per serving).

Total Microwave Cooking Time 12 to 16 Minutes

PROTEIN 45.2 / FAT 12.3 / CARBOHYDRATE 38.0 / SODIUM 1415 / CHOLESTEROL 117

Chicken Normandy

3 tablespoons butter
2 large apples, sliced
1 cup celery, sliced
3 tablespoons cornstarch
1 cup chicken broth
½ cup sweet and sour
   sauce
¼ cup apple juice
¼ cup whipping cream
2 tablespoons apple brandy
½ teaspoon salt
¼ teaspoon pepper
6 (6 oz.) boneless chicken
   breast halves, skinned

In 2-quart oblong glass baking dish, place butter, apples and celery. Microwave at HIGH (10) 5 to 6 minutes. In medium mixing bowl, combine cornstarch, chicken broth, sweet and sour sauce, apple juice, whipping cream and apple brandy. Pour over apples. Microwave at HIGH (10) 8 to 9 minutes, stirring every 3 minutes. Add salt and pepper. Arrange chicken breasts over apples. Cover with vented plastic wrap. Microwave at HIGH (10) 12 to 15 minutes until chicken is thoroughly cooked. Yield: 6 servings (380 calories per serving).

Total Microwave Cooking Time 25 to 30 Minutes

PROTEIN 41.7 / FAT 12.2 / CARBOHYDRATE 22.2 / SODIUM 683 / CHOLESTEROL 128

Chicken & Peppers in White Wine Sauce

½ lb. bacon, chopped
1 (3 lb.) chicken, cut up
1 large onion, coarsely
   chopped
1 large green pepper,
   coarsely chopped
1 large sweet red pepper,
   coarsely chopped
1 teaspoon sage
¼ teaspoon thyme
¼ teaspoon salt
¼ teaspoon pepper
1 (2¼ oz.) can sliced ripe
   olives, drained
1 cup dry white wine

In 3-quart casserole, place bacon and Microwave at HIGH (10) 2 to 3 minutes. Place chicken in casserole, skin side down. Microwave at HIGH (10) 7 minutes; turn over chicken after 4 minutes and drain off fat. Add onion, green pepper, red pepper, sage, thyme, salt, pepper and olives. Stir. Pour wine over chicken. Cover. Microwave at HIGH (10) 9 minutes; stir. Microwave at MEDIUM HIGH (7) 8 to 11 minutes. Yield: 6 servings (663 calories per serving).

Total Microwave Cooking Time 26 to 30 Minutes

PROTEIN 48.9 / FAT 44.9 / CARBOHYDRATE 7.4 / SODIUM 667 / CHOLESTEROL 186

Sauteed Chicken Livers with Wine Sauce

2 tablespoons onion,
   minced
1 clove garlic, minced
3 tablespoons butter
2 tablespoons all-purpose
   flour
1 cup beef broth
3 tablespoons dry red wine
¼ cup all-purpose flour
½ teaspoon garlic salt
¼ teaspoon pepper
1 lb. chicken livers
2 tablespoons butter,
   melted
1 (6 oz.) pkg. long grain
   and wild rice, cooked

In 1½-quart casserole, combine onion, garlic and butter. Microwave at HIGH (10) 2 to 3 minutes until onion is transparent. Add 2 tablespoons flour; stir until smooth. Gradually add beef broth and Microwave at HIGH (10) 2 to 3 minutes until thickened, stirring every minute. Blend in wine and set aside.

In small mixing bowl, combine remaining flour, garlic salt and pepper. Coat chicken livers with flour mixture. Prick chicken livers to prevent bursting. In 2-quart casserole, place 2 tablespoons melted butter and chicken livers. Microwave at HIGH (10) 6 to 8 minutes, turning livers every 2 minutes. Add wine sauce to chicken livers and mix well. Microwave at HIGH (10) 3 to 4 minutes until heated through. Serve over rice. Yield: 4 servings (353 calories per serving).

Total Microwave Cooking Time 13 to 18 Minutes

PROTEIN 24.8 / FAT 18.9 / CARBOHYDRATE 18.0 / SODIUM 930 / CHOLESTEROL 548

Poultry

▲ *Spicy Orange Chicken*

Spicy Orange Chicken

1 teaspoon salt
1 teaspoon paprika
½ teaspoon ginger
¼ teaspoon nutmeg
¼ teaspoon cloves
¼ teaspoon white pepper
1 (2 ½ to 3 lb.) chicken,
   cut up
⅔ cup orange juice
2 tablespoons lemon juice
3 tablespoons brown sugar
1 teaspoon grated
   orange rind
½ cup green onion,
   thinly sliced
1 tablespoon cornstarch
2 tablespoons cold water
1 orange, sliced

Combine salt, paprika, ginger, nutmeg, cloves and pepper. Sprinkle over both sides of chicken. In 2-quart oblong glass baking dish, place chicken with thickest meaty areas to outside edges. Combine orange juice, lemon juice, brown sugar and orange rind. Pour over chicken. Arrange onion slices over chicken. Cover with plastic wrap. Microwave at HIGH (10) 14 to 18 minutes.

Transfer chicken and onion to serving platter; keep warm. Combine cornstarch and water; stir into juices in dish. Microwave at HIGH (10) 2 to 4 minutes until thickened, stirring every minute. Pour over chicken. Garnish with orange slices. Yield: 6 servings (471 calories per serving).

Total Microwave Cooking Time 16 to 22 Minutes

PROTEIN 35.9 / FAT 28.7 / CARBOHYDRATE 15.9 / SODIUM 527 / CHOLESTEROL 142

Garlic Chicken

In shallow dish, combine cornflake crumbs, parsley, garlic powder, salt and pepper; mix well. Place oil in 9-inch pie plate. Dip chicken pieces in oil; coat on both sides with crumb mixture. In 2-quart oblong glass baking dish, place chicken with thickest meaty areas to outside edges. Cover with wax paper. Microwave at HIGH (10) 13 to 17 minutes. Let stand 5 minutes. Yield: 6 servings (598 calories per serving).

Total Microwave Cooking Time 13 to 17 Minutes

PROTEIN 37.6 / FAT 37.6 / CARBOHYDRATE 24.9 / SODIUM 679 / CHOLESTEROL 142

Chicken Waldorf

In 3-quart casserole, place chicken. Combine ½ cup apple juice, lemon juice, ginger, salt, and pepper; pour over chicken. Cover with plastic wrap and microwave at HIGH (10) 12 to 15 minutes. Remove chicken from dish and slice into diagonal slices; keep warm.

Combine remaining apple juice and cornstarch; stir into juices in dish. Microwave at HIGH (10) 3 to 5 minutes until thickened, stirring twice. Stir in apples, celery, raisins, onion and chicken. Microwave at HIGH (10) 3 to 4 minutes until hot. Sprinkle with walnuts. Yield: 6 servings (285 calories per serving).

Total Microwave Cooking Time 18 to 24 Minutes

PROTEIN 40.6 / FAT 5.4 / CARBOHYDRATE 17.6 / SODIUM 229 / CHOLESTEROL 99

Dilly Lemon Chicken

4 (6 oz.) boneless chicken
   breast halves, skinned
¼ cup dry white wine
2 teaspoons lemon juice
1 teaspoon olive oil
¾ teaspoon dillweed
½ teaspoon salt
½ teaspoon lemon pepper
¼ teaspoon tarragon
1 lemon, sliced
2 tablespoons chives,
   chopped
Paprika

Brush chicken breasts with oil. In 2-quart oblong glass baking dish, place chicken. Combine wine, lemon juice, olive oil, dillweed, salt, lemon pepper and tarragon; pour over chicken. Top with lemon slices. Cover with plastic wrap; Microwave at HIGH (10) 10 to 14 minutes, rotating dish ½ turn after 6 minutes. Sprinkle with chives and paprika. Yield: 4 servings (205 calories per serving).

Total Microwave Cooking Time 11 to 14 Minutes

PROTEIN 39.6 / FAT 3.3 / CARBOHYDRATE 2.1 / SODIUM 407 / CHOLESTEROL 99

Poultry

▲ *Turkey Curry*

Turkey Curry

3 tablespoons butter
½ cup onion, chopped
1 medium apple, peeled and coarsely chopped
¼ cup raisins
3 tablespoons all-purpose flour
1 teaspoon curry powder
½ teaspoon coriander
¼ teaspoon cumin
¼ teaspoon ginger
1 cup half & half
1 cup hot water
1 teaspoon instant chicken bouillon granules
3 cups cooked turkey, chopped

In 2-quart casserole, place butter, onion, apple and raisins. Microwave at HIGH (10) 3 to 4 minutes. Add flour, curry powder, coriander, cumin and ginger; stir until smooth. Gradually stir in half & half, water and bouillon. Microwave at HIGH (10) 4 to 6 minutes until thickened, stirring every 2 minutes. Add turkey and Microwave at HIGH (10) 1 to 2 minutes until heated through. Serve over rice. Yield: 6 servings (226 calories per serving).

Total Microwave Cooking Time 8 to 12 Minutes

PROTEIN 14.2 / FAT 12.2 / CARBOHYDRATE 16.3 / SODIUM 954 / CHOLESTEROL 57

Turkey Tetrazzini

¼ cup butter, melted
¼ cup all-purpose flour
1 cup chicken broth
1 cup half & half
4 cups cooked turkey,
   chopped
1 (2 oz.) jar sliced pimento,
   drained
1 (7 oz.) pkg. spaghetti,
   cooked and drained
1 (4 oz.) can sliced
   mushrooms, drained
½ teaspoon salt
½ teaspoon pepper
¼ cup grated
   Parmesan cheese

In 3-quart casserole, combine butter and flour. Gradually add broth and half & half, stirring until smooth. Microwave at MEDIUM HIGH (7) 5 to 6 minutes until thickened, stirring every 2 minutes. Add turkey, pimento, spaghetti, mushrooms, salt and pepper. Sprinkle Parmesan cheese over top. Microwave at HIGH (10) 8 to 10 minutes until thoroughly heated. Yield: 6 servings (325 calories per serving).

Total Microwave Cooking Time 13 to 16 Minutes

PROTEIN 25.2 | FAT 8.7 | CARBOHYDRATE 35.3 | SODIUM 1737 | CHOLESTEROL 53

Turkey with Vegetables

2 tablespoons butter
¼ lb. sliced fresh
   mushrooms
¼ cup carrots,
   thinly sliced
¼ cup celery, sliced
1 lb. cooked turkey,
   thinly sliced
¼ cup white wine
¼ cup chicken broth
1 tablespoon parsley,
   snipped
1½ teaspoons cornstarch
¼ teaspoon salt
⅛ teaspoon pepper

In 2-quart casserole, combine butter, mushrooms, carrots and celery. Microwave at HIGH (10) 3 to 4 minutes. Add turkey slices and Microwave at HIGH (10) 5 to 6 minutes until turkey is heated through. Combine wine, broth, parsley, cornstarch, salt and pepper; pour over turkey. Stir to coat. Microwave at HIGH (10) 2 to 3 minutes, stirring every minute. Yield: 4 servings (207 calories per serving).

Total Microwave Cooking Time 10 to 13 Minutes

PROTEIN 21.9 | FAT 8.6 | CARBOHYDRATE 9.0 | SODIUM 1489 | CHOLESTEROL 60

Turkey Stroganoff

3 tablespoons melted
   butter, divided
¼ teaspoon salt
¼ teaspoon pepper
4 cups cooked turkey,
   cubed
1 medium onion, sliced
1 cup fresh mushrooms,
   sliced
2 medium zucchini, sliced
1 tablespoon all-purpose
   flour
1 cup chicken broth
½ teaspoon basil
1 (8 oz.) carton sour cream
2 teaspoons dry mustard

In 3-quart casserole, place 2 tablespoons butter, salt and pepper. Toss turkey pieces in butter. Microwave at HIGH (10) 5 to 7 minutes; stir after 3 minutes. Add onion, mushrooms and zucchini to turkey. Microwave at HIGH (10) 4 to 6 minutes; stir after 2 minutes.

In 4-cup glass measure, combine 1 tablespoon melted butter and flour. Add chicken broth and basil; stir well. Microwave at HIGH (10) 3 to 5 minutes, stirring every minute. Add sour cream and mustard; stir to blend. Pour over turkey and vegetables. Microwave at HIGH (10) 2 to 4 minutes until heated through. Serve over rice or noodles. Yield: 6 servings (264 calories per serving).

Total Microwave Cooking Time 14 to 22 Minutes

PROTEIN 20.4 | FAT 16.6 | CARBOHYDRATE 9.8 | SODIUM 1354 | CHOLESTEROL 67

Fish & Seafood

Baked Lobster Tails

4 (8 oz.) lobster tails,
  thawed
3 tablespoons butter,
  melted
⅓ cup seasoned dry
  bread crumbs
⅛ teaspoon onion powder
⅛ teaspoon paprika
⅛ teaspoon salt

With kitchen shears, cut lobster through center of soft shell (underneath) to the tail. Lift lobster out of shell by loosening with fingers, leaving meat attached to tail section. (Lobster meat will rest on shell.) Arrange in 10-inch glass pie plate, tails toward center. In small mixing bowl, combine butter, bread crumbs, onion powder, paprika and salt; sprinkle over lobster. Cover with wax paper. Microwave at MEDIUM HIGH (7) 9 to 13 minutes until lobster is done. Let stand 5 minutes. Serve with Lemon Butter, if desired. Yield: 4 servings (314 calories per serving).

Lemon Butter: In small bowl, Microwave ½ cup butter and 1 to 2 tablespoons lemon juice at MEDIUM (5) 1 to 2 minutes until butter is melted.

Total Microwave Cooking Time 9 to 13 Minutes

PROTEIN 43.8 / FAT 11.1 / CARBOHYDRATE 7.3 / SODIUM 223 / CHOLESTEROL 239

Italian Haddock

2 tablespoons olive oil
1 tablespoon lemon juice
1 cup tomatoes, chopped
1½ cups fresh mushrooms,
  sliced
¼ cup onion, chopped
¼ cup green pepper,
  chopped
2 tablespoons fresh
  parsley, snipped
¾ teaspoon oregano
½ teaspoon seasoned salt
¼ teaspoon garlic powder
1 (16 oz.) pkg. frozen
  haddock fillets, thawed
Dash pepper

In 2-quart casserole, combine olive oil, lemon juice, tomatoes, mushrooms, onion, green pepper, parsley, oregano, seasoned salt and garlic powder. Cover. Microwave at HIGH (10) 4 to 6 minutes until onion is tender; stir after 2 minutes.

Place fish fillets in 2-quart oblong glass baking dish; sprinkle with pepper. Spoon vegetable mixture over fillets. Cover with vented plastic wrap. Microwave at HIGH (10) 2 to 4 minutes until fish flakes easily when tested with a fork. Let stand 2 to 3 minutes. Yield: 4 servings (186 calories per serving).

Total Microwave Cooking Time 6 to 10 Minutes

PROTEIN 22.9 / FAT 7.9 / CARBOHYDRATE 5.8 / SODIUM 471 / CHOLESTEROL 65

Salmon Loaf

2 (16 oz.) cans red salmon,
  drained with bone and
  skin removed
¾ cup dry bread crumbs
½ cup milk
1 egg, beaten
¼ cup butter, melted
½ teaspoon salt
2 tablespoons grated
  Parmesan cheese

In large mixing bowl, combine salmon, bread crumbs, milk, egg, butter, salt and Parmesan cheese. Mix well. Pack mixture firmly into 8x4x3-inch glass loaf dish. Microwave at MEDIUM HIGH (7) 14 to 18 minutes. Yield: 6 servings (335 calories per serving).

Total Microwave Cooking Time 14 to 18 Minutes

PROTEIN 33.7 / FAT 20.9 / CARBOHYDRATE 1.3 / SODIUM 1143 / CHOLESTEROL 134

Fish & Seafood

▲ *Salmon Steaks*

Sprinkle lemon pepper onto buttered dish for extra flavor.

Salmon Steaks

1 tablespoon butter
2 teaspoons lemon pepper
6 (5 oz.) salmon steaks
2 teaspoons lemon juice
1 teaspoon lemon pepper
½ teaspoon garlic powder
6 thin onion slices
3 lemon slices, halved
1 teaspoon tarragon
1 teaspoon paprika
Dash salt

Place butter in 2-quart oblong glass baking dish. Microwave at HIGH (10) 30 seconds to 1 minute until melted. Coat bottom of dish with butter and sprinkle with 2 teaspoons lemon pepper. Place salmon steaks in prepared dish. Combine lemon juice, 1 teaspoon lemon pepper and garlic powder. Brush over salmon steaks. Place one onion slice and one lemon slice on each salmon steak. Sprinkle with tarragon, paprika and salt. Microwave at HIGH (10) 8 to 10 minutes until fish flakes easily when tested with a fork. Yield: 6 servings (273 calories per serving).

Total Microwave Cooking Time 8½ to 11 Minutes

PROTEIN 30.9 / FAT 14.2 / CARBOHYDRATE 4.3 / SODIUM 307 / CHOLESTEROL 93

Shrimp with Dill Sauce

2 tablespoons onion, chopped
1 tablespoon butter
1½ lbs. medium shrimp, uncooked, peeled and deveined
¼ cup white wine
3 tablespoons butter, melted
3 tablespoons all-purpose flour
1 cup milk
3 tablespoons lemon juice
1 teaspoon dillweed .
¼ teaspoon garlic salt

In 2-quart casserole, place onion and butter. Microwave at HIGH (10) 1 to 2 minutes until onion is tender. Add shrimp and wine. Microwave at HIGH (10) 5 to 6 minutes, stirring every 2 minutes.

In medium bowl, combine melted butter and flour, stirring until smooth. Gradually add milk, stirring constantly. Microwave at HIGH (10) 3 to 4 minutes, stirring after 2 minutes. Add lemon juice, dillweed and garlic salt. Pour over shrimp mixture. Mix well. Microwave at HIGH (10) 3 to 5 minutes, stirring after 2 minutes. Serve over rice. Yield: 6 servings (238 calories per serving).

Total Microwave Cooking Time 12 to 17 Minutes

PROTEIN 25.0 / FAT 11.1 / CARBOHYDRATE 7.0 / SODIUM 368 / CHOLESTEROL 199

Fish Almondine

½ cup slivered almonds
½ cup butter
1 lb. fish fillets
1 teaspoon lemon juice
1 teaspoon fresh parsley,
  snipped
¼ teaspoon dillweed
¼ teaspoon salt
⅛ teaspoon pepper

In 8-inch square glass baking dish, place almonds and butter. Microwave at HIGH (10) 5 to 6 minutes until almonds are golden brown. Remove almonds and set aside. Place fish in baking dish, turning to coat both sides with butter. Sprinkle with lemon juice, parsley, dillweed, salt, pepper and almonds. Cover with wax paper. Microwave at HIGH (10) 4 to 6 minutes until fish flakes easily when tested with a fork. Let stand 1 minute before serving. Yield: 3 servings (565 calories per serving).

Total Microwave Cooking Time 9 to 12 Minutes

PROTEIN 34.3 / FAT 46.9 / CARBOHYDRATE 4.4 / SODIUM 815 / CHOLESTEROL 169

Seafood Marinara

2 tablespoons butter,
  melted
¼ teaspoon garlic powder
2 tomatoes, peeled and
  chopped
1 tablespoon tomato paste
¼ cup white wine
2 teaspoons fresh parsley,
  snipped
¾ teaspoon basil
¼ teaspoon lemon pepper
½ lb. scallops
½ lb. shrimp, uncooked,
  peeled and deveined

In 1-quart casserole, combine butter, garlic powder, tomatoes, tomato paste, wine, parsley, basil and lemon pepper. Microwave at HIGH (10) 5 to 6 minutes; stir after 3 minutes. Puree tomato mixture in blender at high speed for 1 minute.

In 2-quart casserole, place scallops and shrimp. Add tomato mixture. Microwave at HIGH (10) 5 to 7 minutes. Let stand 5 minutes. Serve over pasta. Yield: 4 servings (187 calories per serving).

Total Microwave Cooking Time 10 to 13 Minutes

PROTEIN 21.7 / FAT 7.4 / CARBOHYDRATE 5.6 / SODIUM 265 / CHOLESTEROL 120

Scalloped Oysters

2 tablespoons butter
½ cup onion, chopped
½ cup green pepper,
  chopped
¼ cup butter, melted
2 cups buttery cracker
  crumbs
½ teaspoon salt
⅛ teaspoon pepper
2 (8 oz.) cans fresh oysters,
  drained
1 cup evaporated milk
1 teaspoon
  Worcestershire sauce

In 1-quart casserole, place butter, onion and green pepper. Microwave at HIGH (10) 3 to 4 minutes until tender. Set aside. In small mixing bowl, combine butter, cracker crumbs, salt and pepper. Mix well.

In 1½-quart casserole, place ⅓ crumb mixture, one can of oysters and half of onion and green pepper mixture. Repeat layers ending with cracker crumbs.

In small mixing bowl, combine evaporated milk and Worcestershire sauce; pour over layered casserole. Cover with plastic wrap; vent. Microwave at HIGH (10) 6 minutes. Remove plastic wrap and rotate dish ½ turn. Microwave at HIGH (10) 6 to 8 minutes until done. Yield: 6 servings (313 calories per serving).

Total Microwave Cooking Time 15 to 18 Minutes

PROTEIN 7.9 / FAT 22.1 / CARBOHYDRATE 20.3 / SODIUM 662 / CHOLESTEROL 80

Fish & Seafood

▲ *Scallops Oriental*

Scallops Oriental

1 lb. fresh scallops
½ cup water
1½ cups carrots,
    thinly sliced
2 tablespoons green onion,
    sliced
¼ teaspoon garlic powder
1 tablespoon oil
1 tablespoon cornstarch
¾ teaspoon sugar
½ teaspoon ground ginger
½ cup chicken broth
2 tablespoons soy sauce
2 tablespoons dry sherry
1 (6 oz.) pkg. frozen
    snow peas, thawed

In 2-quart casserole, place scallops and water. Cover. Microwave at HIGH (10) 4 to 7 minutes until scallops are opaque, stirring every 2 minutes. Drain and set aside.

In 2-quart casserole, combine carrots, green onion, garlic powder and oil. Cover. Microwave at HIGH (10) 3 to 6 minutes until vegetables are crisp-tender. Stir in cornstarch, sugar, ginger, chicken broth, soy sauce and sherry. Microwave at HIGH (10) 2 to 3 minutes until thickened, stirring every minute. Add snow peas. Microwave at HIGH (10) 2 to 3 minutes until snow peas are crisp-tender, stirring every minute. Add scallops. Microwave at HIGH (10) 2 to 3 minutes until heated through. Stir after 2 minutes. Yield: 4 servings (219 calories per serving).

Total Microwave Cooking Time 13 to 22 Minutes

PROTEIN 23.2 / FAT 4.9 / CARBOHYDRATE 18.3 / SODIUM 825 / CHOLESTEROL 38

Baked Fish with Cheese

1 lb. thin fish fillets
1 tablespoon tarragon
½ teaspoon seasoned salt
2 tablespoons butter
¼ cup sour cream
1 cup mozzarella cheese,
    shredded

Arrange fish in 2-quart oblong glass baking dish. Sprinkle with tarragon and seasoned salt. Dot with butter; cover with wax paper. Microwave at HIGH (10) 3 to 5 minutes. Set aside. In small mixing bowl, blend sour cream and mozzarella cheese. Spread mixture on fish and cover with wax paper. Microwave at HIGH (10) 3 to 5 minutes. Yield: 3 servings (358 calories per serving).

Total Microwave Cooking Time 6 to 10 Minutes

PROTEIN 37.7 / FAT 21.4 / CARBOHYDRATE 2.6 / SODIUM 618 / CHOLESTEROL 195

Tuna Salad Deluxe

2 (6 ½ oz.) cans water-pack tuna, drained
1 cup celery, chopped
½ cup onion, chopped
⅓ cup ripe olives, sliced
½ cup sour cream
½ cup mayonnaise
1 tablespoon lemon juice
¼ teaspoon thyme
¼ teaspoon pepper
½ cup Swiss cheese, shredded
½ cup sliced almonds

In 2-quart casserole, combine tuna, celery, onion, olives, sour cream, mayonnaise, lemon juice, thyme and pepper; cover. Microwave at MEDIUM HIGH (7) 7 to 11 minutes, stirring after 5 minutes. Sprinkle with cheese and almonds. Microwave at MEDIUM HIGH (7) 1 to 3 minutes until cheese melts. Yield: 6 servings (372 calories per serving).

Total Microwave Cooking Time 8 to 14 Minutes

PROTEIN 23.4 / FAT 28.6 / CARBOHYDRATE 6.2 / SODIUM 483 / CHOLESTEROL 56

Coquille St. Jacques

3 tablespoons butter
1 (4½ oz.) jar sliced mushrooms
¼ cup celery, chopped
2 green onions, sliced
2 tablespoons all-purpose flour
½ teaspoon thyme
½ teaspoon salt
¼ teaspoon white pepper
⅓ cup white wine
1 lb. scallops
1 (2 oz.) jar sliced pimento, drained
¼ cup half & half
1 egg yolk, beaten
½ cup dry bread crumbs
2 tablespoons grated Parmesan cheese

In 2-quart casserole, place butter, mushrooms, celery and onions. Microwave at HIGH (10) 2 to 3 minutes until butter is melted; stir well. Add flour, thyme, salt and pepper; add wine, stirring until smooth. Stir in scallops and pimento. Microwave at HIGH (10) 4 to 6 minutes until thickened, stirring after 2 minutes. Stir in half & half and egg yolk. Microwave at MEDIUM (5) 2 to 4 minutes, stirring after 1 minute.

Divide mixture among 4 scallop shells. Combine bread crumbs and cheese; sprinkle evenly over scallop mixture. Cover with wax paper. Microwave at MEDIUM HIGH (7) 4 to 7 minutes until hot. Yield: 4 servings (287 calories per serving).

Total Microwave Cooking Time 12 to 20 Minutes

PROTEIN 23.4 / FAT 13.7 / CARBOHYDRATE 13.9 / SODIUM 791 / CHOLESTEROL 123

Far-East Fish Fillets

4 (6 oz.) orange roughy fillets
¼ cup soy sauce
¼ cup orange juice
¼ teaspoon ginger
1 clove garlic, minced
½ cup fresh mushrooms, sliced
½ cup celery, chopped
½ cup sweet red pepper, chopped

In 8-inch square glass baking dish, place fish. Combine soy sauce, orange juice, ginger and garlic; pour over fish. Cover and let stand in refrigerator 1 hour; turn fillets over after 30 minutes. Drain and discard marinade. Spread mushrooms, celery and red pepper over fish. Cover with vented plastic wrap. Microwave at HIGH (10) 8 to 10 minutes until fish flakes easily when tested with a fork. Yield: 4 servings (241 calories per serving).

Total Microwave Cooking Time 8 to 10 Minutes

PROTEIN 26.5 / FAT 12.1 / CARBOHYDRATE 5.3 / SODIUM 950 / CHOLESTEROL 34

Fish & Seafood

▲ *Creamy Crabmeat and Almonds*

Creamy Crabmeat and Almonds

½ cup fresh mushrooms,
  sliced
1 small green pepper,
  cut in thin strips
2 tablespoons butter
2 (6 oz.) cans crabmeat,
  drained
⅓ cup slivered almonds
1 tablespoon orange juice
1 teaspoon lemon juice
2 (10 ½ oz.) cans
  cream of celery soup
¾ teaspoon celery salt
⅓ cup ripe olives,
  quartered
1 (4 oz.) jar sliced
  pimento, drained
2 tablespoons fresh
  parsley, snipped
¼ teaspoon hot sauce

In 2-quart casserole, combine mushrooms, green pepper and butter. Microwave at HIGH (10) 2 to 3 minutes until mushrooms are tender. Add crabmeat, almonds, orange juice, lemon juice, celery soup, celery salt, olives, pimento, parsley and hot sauce; cover. Microwave at HIGH (10) 8 to 12 minutes; stir after 6 minutes. Let stand, covered, 5 minutes. Serve over rice. Yield: 8 servings (387 calories per serving).

Total Microwave Cooking Time 10 to 15 Minutes

PROTEIN 18.2 / FAT 13.4 / CARBOHYDRATE 57.2 / SODIUM 1345 / CHOLESTEROL 39

Shrimp Pilaf

¼ cup butter
½ cup onion,
   thinly sliced
⅓ cup green pepper, diced
2 cups instant rice
2 cups hot water
2 (8 oz.) cans tomato sauce
1 ½ teaspoons seasoned
   salt
¼ teaspoon pepper
¼ teaspoon prepared
   mustard
2 (4 ¼ oz.) cans shrimp,
   drained

In 2-quart casserole, place butter, onion and green pepper. Microwave at HIGH (10) 4 to 5 minutes; stir after 2 minutes. Add rice, water, tomato sauce, seasoned salt, pepper, mustard and shrimp; mix well. Cover. Microwave at HIGH (10) 9 to 11 minutes, stirring every 3 minutes. Yield: 6 servings (374 calories per serving).

Total Microwave Cooking Time 13 to 16 Minutes

PROTEIN 15.1 / FAT 9.1 / CARBOHYDRATE 57.4 / SODIUM 1050 / CHOLESTEROL 90

Scallops In Wine Sauce

½ cup water
¾ lb. scallops
3 tablespoons butter
½ teaspoon garlic powder
2 green onions, chopped
¼ teaspoon paprika
2 tablespoons dry
   white wine
1 tablespoon lemon juice

In 1½-quart casserole, place water and scallops. Cover. Microwave at HIGH (10) 3 to 5 minutes until scallops are opaque; stir after 2 minutes. Drain and set aside.

In 2-cup glass measure, combine butter, garlic powder, onions, paprika, wine and lemon juice. Microwave at HIGH (10) 2 to 4 minutes. Pour over scallops. Yield: 2 servings (322 calories per serving).

Total Microwave Cooking Time 5 to 9 Minutes

PROTEIN 29.2 / FAT 18.7 / CARBOHYDRATE 6.6 / SODIUM 457 / CHOLESTEROL 103

Garden-Style Swordfish

2 medium carrots,
   shredded
1 small onion, sliced
1 medium zucchini, sliced
¼ cup celery, chopped
4 (6 oz.) swordfish steaks
2 tablespoons butter,
   melted
1 tablespoon lemon juice
½ teaspoon salt
½ teaspoon rosemary
¼ teaspoon marjoram
4 lemon slices

Combine carrots, onion, zucchini and celery. In 2-quart oblong glass baking dish, spread vegetable mixture evenly. Arrange fish steaks over vegetables. Combine butter, lemon juice, salt, rosemary and marjoram; drizzle over fish. Top each fish steak with lemon slice. Cover with vented plastic wrap. Microwave at HIGH (10) 11 to 14 minutes until fish flakes easily when tested with a fork. Yield: 4 servings (291 calories per serving).

Total Microwave Cooking Time 11 to 14 Minutes

PROTEIN 34.9 / FAT 12.8 / CARBOHYDRATE 8.2 / SODIUM 526 / CHOLESTEROL 82

Casseroles

Vegetable Lasagna

1 large onion,
   finely chopped
1 cup carrots, shredded
1 (4½ oz.) jar sliced
   mushrooms, drained
1 (16 oz.) carton small curd
   cottage cheese
1 egg, beaten
¼ cup grated
   Parmesan cheese
1 teaspoon oregano
1 (14 oz.) jar spaghetti
   sauce, divided
6 no boil lasagna noodles
1 (10 oz.) pkg. frozen
   chopped spinach,
   thawed and well drained
1 cup tomatos, peeled
   and coarsely chopped
2 cups mozzarella cheese,
   shredded

In 1½-quart casserole, combine onion, carrots and mushrooms; cover. Microwave at HIGH (10) 3 to 4 minutes until tender; drain and set aside. In small mixing bowl, combine cottage cheese, egg, Parmesan cheese and oregano; set aside.

In 2-quart oblong glass baking dish, layer half of spaghetti sauce, 3 lasagna noodles, all of onion-carrot-mushroom mixture and half of cheese mixture.

Cover with remaining noodles, spaghetti sauce, spinach and cheese mixture. Top with tomatoes and mozzarella cheese. Microwave at HIGH (10) 16 to 20 minutes. Yield: 8 servings (247 calories per serving).

Total Microwave Cooking Time 19 to 24 Minutes

PROTEIN 18.3 / FAT 11.6 / CARBOHYDRATE 18.8 / SODIUM 695 / CHOLESTEROL 65

Spread half of cheese mixture over mixed vegetables to form first layer.

Form the second layer with remaining ingredients, starting with the noodles.

Yellow Squash Casserole

4 cups yellow squash,
   sliced
½ cup water
1 dozen buttery crackers,
   crushed
1 (3 oz.) pkg. cream
   cheese, softened
1 (10 ¾ oz.) can cream of
   chicken soup
1 egg
¼ cup butter, melted
3 small carrots, grated
½ cup onion,
   finely chopped
½ cup herb-seasoned
   stuffing mix

In 2-quart casserole, combine squash and water. Cover. Microwave at HIGH (10) 8 minutes; stir after 4 minutes. Drain and coarsely chop.

Place crackers in greased 2-quart oblong glass baking dish. In medium mixing bowl, combine cream cheese, soup, egg and butter. Beat with electric mixer at high speed for 1 minute. Stir in squash, carrots and onion. Spoon into prepared baking dish. Microwave at HIGH (10) 12 to 14 minutes. Sprinkle with stuffing mix. Microwave at HIGH (10) 4 to 5 minutes. Let stand 5 minutes. Yield: 8 servings (225 calories per serving).

Total Microwave Cooking Time 24 to 27 Minutes

PROTEIN 5.2 / FAT 14.6 / CARBOHYDRATE 19.4 / SODIUM 598 / CHOLESTEROL 63

Casseroles

▲ *Chicken Enchiladas*

Chicken Enchiladas

3 (5 oz.) cans cooked chicken
1 cup sour cream
1 (10 ¾ oz.) can cream of chicken soup
¾ cup Monterey Jack cheese, shredded
¾ cup Colby cheese, shredded
2 tablespoons chopped green chilies
¼ cup onion, chopped
¼ teaspoon pepper
6 (8-inch) flour tortillas
½ cup Colby cheese, shredded

In large mixing bowl, combine chicken, sour cream, soup, cheeses, green chilies, onion and pepper. Mix well. Place ¾ cup of mixture on each tortilla; roll up and place seam side down in 2-quart oblong glass baking dish. Sprinkle with ½ cup Colby cheese. Microwave at HIGH (10) 10 to 14 minutes. Yield: 6 servings (525 calories per serving).

Total Microwave Cooking Time 10 to 14 Minutes

PROTEIN 34.8 / FAT 30.4 / CARBOHYDRATE 29.2 / SODIUM 700 / CHOLESTEROL 117

Creamed Spaghetti with Turkey Casserole

1¼ cups spaghetti, broken
   into 2-inch pieces
1½ cups cooked turkey,
   cubed
⅓ cup onion, chopped
⅓ cup water
¼ cup green pepper,
   chopped
1 (2 oz.) jar sliced pimento
1 (10¾ oz.) can cream of
   mushroom soup
¼ teaspoon salt
¼ teaspoon pepper
2 cups Cheddar cheese,
   shredded

Cook spaghetti according to directions in chart on page 117; drain.

In 2-quart oblong glass baking dish, combine cooked spaghetti, turkey, onion, water, green pepper, pimento, soup, salt, pepper and cheese. Mix well. Microwave at MEDIUM HIGH (7) 15 to 21 minutes. Yield: 6 servings (304 calories per serving).

Total Microwave Cooking Time 15 to 21 Minutes

PROTEIN 21.6 / FAT 17.6 / CARBOHYDRATE 14.1 / SODIUM 776 / CHOLESTEROL 63

Vegetable-Stuffed Eggplant

1 medium eggplant
2 medium tomatoes,
   seeded and chopped
½ cup green pepper,
   chopped
½ cup celery, sliced
½ cup onion, chopped
1 cup buttery cracker
   crumbs
¼ teaspoon salt
⅛ teaspoon pepper
¼ cup water
½ cup Cheddar cheese,
   shredded

Cut eggplant in half lengthwise. Scoop out pulp, leaving ¼-inch thick shell. Dice eggplant pulp. In 1½-quart casserole, combine diced eggplant, tomatoes, green pepper, celery and onion; cover. Microwave at HIGH (10) 4 minutes, stirring after 2 minutes; drain. Add cracker crumbs, salt and pepper; blend well. Divide mixture evenly between eggplant shells. Place shells in 2-quart oblong glass baking dish; add water. Cover with vented plastic wrap. Microwave at HIGH (10) 4 to 7 minutes; rotate dish ½ turn after 3 minutes. Sprinkle with cheese and let stand 5 minutes. Yield: 6 servings (142 calories per serving).

Total Microwave Cooking Time 8 to 11 Minutes

PROTEIN 3.7 / FAT 7.4 / CARBOHYDRATE 16.0 / SODIUM 296 / CHOLESTEROL 10

Scoop out eggplant leaving the outer shell intact and dice the insides to be used in the stuffing.

Spicy Wild Rice Casserole

1 lb. hot bulk sausage
½ cup celery, chopped
½ cup onion, chopped
½ cup fresh mushrooms,
   sliced
½ cup green pepper,
   chopped
1½ cups water
1 (10¾ oz.) can cream of
   mushroom soup
1 (6 oz.) pkg. long grain
   and wild rice
1 cup Cheddar cheese,
   shredded

In 2-quart casserole, combine sausage, celery, onion, mushrooms and green pepper; cover. Microwave at HIGH (10) 6 to 10 minutes, stirring every 3 minutes. Drain. Add water, soup, rice and cheese. Cover. Microwave at HIGH (10) 16 to 22 minutes. Stir after 10 minutes. Let stand 5 minutes. Yield: 6 servings (437 calories per serving).

Total Microwave Cooking Time 22 to 32 Minutes

PROTEIN 12.9 / FAT 28.6 / CARBOHYDRATE 31.9 / SODIUM 1344 / CHOLESTEROL 55

Casseroles

▲ *Simple Tuna Casserole*

Toss bread cubes in melted butter until coated evenly.

Simple Tuna Casserole

3 tablespoons butter
2 tablespoons onion, chopped
3 tablespoons all-purpose flour
1 teaspoon salt
¼ teaspoon pepper
1½ cups milk
2 (6½ oz.) cans tuna, drained
2 cups soft bread cubes
2 tablespoons butter, melted
1 (10 oz.) pkg. frozen peas, thawed
1 medium carrot, shredded
1 cup sharp Cheddar cheese, shredded

In 2-quart casserole, place butter and onion. Microwave at HIGH (10) 1 to 3 minutes until onion is transparent. Add flour, salt, pepper and milk. Stir well to blend. Microwave at HIGH (10) 4 to 6 minutes until thickened, stirring every 2 minutes. Add tuna.

In 8-inch square glass baking dish, toss bread cubes in melted butter. Add peas and carrot. Pour cream sauce over vegetables and top with cheese. Microwave at HIGH (10) 9 to 13 minutes. Yield: 6 servings (470 calories per serving).

Total Microwave Cooking Time 14 to 22 Minutes

PROTEIN 30.3 / FAT 21.1 / CARBOHYDRATE 38.8 / SODIUM 1167 / CHOLESTEROL 82

Hamburger & Zucchini Casserole

1½ lbs. lean ground beef
1 medium onion, chopped
1 (14½ oz.) can tomatoes
1 (15 oz.) can tomato sauce
½ teaspoon garlic powder
½ teaspoon salt
¼ teaspoon pepper
1 (15¼ oz.) can whole kernel corn, drained
3 small zucchini, diced

In 3-quart casserole, combine beef and onion. Microwave at HIGH (10) 4 to 7 minutes; stir after 3 minutes. Drain. Add tomatoes, tomato sauce, garlic powder, salt, pepper, corn and zucchini. Stir well. Cover. Microwave at HIGH (10) 15 to 23 minutes; stir after 9 minutes. Let stand, covered, 5 minutes. Yield: 6 servings (344 calories per serving).

Total Microwave Cooking Time 19 to 30 Minutes

PROTEIN 20.0 / FAT 18.6 / CARBOHYDRATE 27.4 / SODIUM 977 / CHOLESTEROL 64

Enchilada Casserole

1½ lbs. lean ground beef
1 medium onion, chopped
1 (8 oz.) can tomato sauce
1 (12 oz.) can Mexicorn,
  drained
1 (2¼ oz.) can sliced ripe
  olives, drained
1 (10 oz.) can hot
  enchilada sauce
½ teaspoon salt
½ teaspoon oregano
¼ teaspoon chili powder
¼ teaspoon pepper
6 corn tortillas, divided
2 cups Cheddar cheese,
  shredded, divided

In 2-quart casserole, combine ground beef and onion. Cover. Microwave at HIGH (10) 6 to 10 minutes until meat is thoroughly cooked; stir after 5 minutes. Drain. Add tomato sauce, corn, ripe olives, enchilada sauce, salt, oregano, chili powder and pepper. Microwave at HIGH (10) 3 to 5 minutes.

Place 3 tortillas in bottom of 2-quart oblong glass baking dish. Pour half of meat mixture over tortillas. Sprinkle 1 cup of cheese on top. Repeat layers. Microwave at HIGH (10) 9 to 15 minutes. Yield: 6 servings (669 calories per serving).

Total Microwave Cooking Time 18 to 30 Minutes

PROTEIN 35.6 / FAT 40.9 / CARBOHYDRATE 40.9 / SODIUM 1297 / CHOLESTEROL 125

Place 6 tortillas in dish to start first layer.

Sprinkle first layer with cheese and repeat layers.

Cheesy Chicken Casserole

¼ cup butter
½ cup fresh mushrooms,
  sliced
⅛ cup green pepper,
  chopped
¼ cup onion, chopped
6 tablespoons all-purpose
  flour
1 (14½ oz.) can chicken
  broth
1 cup milk
½ teaspoon salt
⅛ teaspoon pepper
1 (8 oz.) pkg. medium egg
  noodles, cooked
3 (5 oz.) cans cooked
  chicken
1 cup Cheddar cheese,
  shredded

In 3-quart casserole, combine butter, mushrooms, green pepper and onion. Cover with vented plastic wrap. Microwave at HIGH (10) 3 to 6 minutes until tender, stirring every 2 minutes. Add flour, chicken broth, milk, salt and pepper. Stir well. Microwave at HIGH (10) 3 to 6 minutes, stirring with wire whisk every 2 minutes. Add noodles and chicken. Top with Cheddar cheese. Microwave at HIGH (10) 9 to 15 minutes until heated through. Yield: 6 servings (556 calories per serving).

Total Microwave Cooking Time 15 to 27 Minutes

PROTEIN 37.3 / FAT 22.3 / CARBOHYDRATE 49.8 / SODIUM 880 / CHOLESTEROL 110

Beef and Vegetable Supper

1 lb. lean ground beef
2 medium potatoes,
  thinly sliced
2 medium carrots,
  thinly sliced
⅓ cup long grain rice
2 small onions, sliced
1 (28 oz.) can tomatoes
2 tablespoons brown sugar

In 2-quart casserole, place beef; cover. Microwave at HIGH (10) 5 to 7 minutes until browned; stir after 3 minutes. Remove from casserole and drain well. In same casserole, layer potatoes, carrots, rice, onions, ground beef and tomatoes. Sprinkle with brown sugar. Microwave at HIGH (10) 15 to 23 minutes until vegetables are tender. Yield: 4 servings (458 calories per serving).

Total Microwave Cooking Time 20 to 30 Minutes

PROTEIN 21.1 / FAT 18.3 / CARBOHYDRATE 52.7 / SODIUM 405 / CHOLESTEROL 64

Casseroles

Noodles Con Carne

Wear gloves when chopping hot peppers to protect from burning reaction.

1 lb. lean ground beef
½ cup green pepper, chopped
¼ cup onion, chopped
⅛ teaspoon pepper
1 hot pepper, chopped, optional
1 (15 oz.) can chili beans
1 (8 oz.) can tomato sauce
2 cups Cheddar cheese, shredded
6 oz. wide egg noodles, cooked and drained
1½ tablespoons chili powder

In 3-quart casserole, crumble ground beef, green pepper, onion, pepper and hot pepper. Microwave at HIGH (10) 6 to 10 minutes until meat is browned and onion is tender, stirring every 3 minutes. Drain. Add chili beans, tomato sauce, Cheddar cheese, noodles and chili powder; mix well. Microwave at HIGH (10) 9 to 15 minutes until bubbly. Yield: 8 servings (403 calories per serving).

Total Microwave Cooking Time 15 to 25 Minutes

PROTEIN 22.1 / FAT 19.8 / CARBOHYDRATE 33.9 / SODIUM 572 / CHOLESTEROL 91

Lasagna

1 lb. lean ground beef
½ cup onion, chopped
2 (8 oz.) cans tomato sauce
1 (6 oz.) can tomato paste
1¾ teaspoons basil
1½ teaspoons oregano
1 teaspoon parsley flakes
¾ teaspoon garlic salt
1 (16 oz.) carton small curd cottage cheese
1 egg, beaten
6 no boil lasagna noodles
2 cups mozzarella cheese, shredded, divided
½ cup grated Parmesan cheese

In 2-quart casserole, place beef and onion. Cover. Microwave at HIGH (10) 5 to 7 minutes until beef is thoroughly cooked; stir after 3 minutes. Drain. Add tomato sauce, tomato paste, basil, oregano, parsley flakes and garlic salt. Set aside. In small mixing bowl, combine cottage cheese and egg. Set aside.

In 2-quart oblong glass baking dish, spread ⅛ of meat sauce over bottom. Top with half of lasagna noodles, half of cottage cheese mixture and half of mozzarella cheese. Repeat layers, ending with meat sauce. Sprinkle with Parmesan cheese. Microwave at MEDIUM (5) 30 to 38 minutes. Yield: 8 servings (341 calories per serving).

Total Microwave Cooking Time 35 to 45 Minutes

PROTEIN 24.1 / FAT 19.6 / CARBOHYDRATE 17.5 / SODIUM 963 / CHOLESTEROL 97

Hearty Bean Casserole

1½ lbs. lean ground beef
½ cup catsup
¼ cup dark molasses
2 tablespoons vinegar
⅓ cup onion, minced
1 (17 oz.) can lima beans, drained
1 (15½ oz.) can red kidney beans, drained
1 (16 oz.) can pork and beans
1 (8 oz.) can tomato sauce
½ teaspoon dry mustard

In 3-quart casserole, place ground beef. Microwave at HIGH (10) 5 to 7 minutes until beef is thoroughly cooked, stirring every 2 minutes. Drain. Add catsup, molasses, vinegar, onion, lima beans, kidney beans, pork and beans, tomato sauce and dry mustard. Microwave at MEDIUM HIGH (7) 12 to 18 minutes; stir after 8 minutes. Yield: 10 servings (304 calories per serving).

Total Microwave Cooking Time 17 to 25 Minutes

PROTEIN 17.0 / FAT 11.5 / CARBOHYDRATE 34.6 / SODIUM 789 / CHOLESTEROL 41

Layered Zucchini Bake

1 cup small curd cottage
    cheese, drained
1 cup Monterey Jack
    cheese, shredded
1 teaspoon parsley flakes
½ teaspoon chili powder
½ teaspoon garlic salt
¼ teaspoon cumin
3 medium zucchini
1 large tomato, sliced
½ cup grated Romano
    cheese

In small bowl, combine cottage cheese, Monterey Jack cheese, parsley, chili powder, garlic salt and cumin; set aside.

Slice zucchini lengthwise into ⅛-inch strips. Place in 8-inch square glass baking dish; cover with wax paper. Microwave at HIGH (10) 6 to 10 minutes until tender; rearrange after 3 minutes. Discard cooking liquid and drain zucchini on paper towels. Return half of zucchini to baking dish. Spread cottage cheese mixture over zucchini. Arrange remaining zucchini over cottage cheese. Top with tomato slices. Sprinkle with Romano cheese. Microwave at MEDIUM (5) 18 to 25 minutes. Let stand 5 minutes. Yield: 6 servings (159 calories per serving).

Total Microwave Cooking Time 24 to 35 Minutes

PROTEIN 13.2 / FAT 10.2 / CARBOHYDRATE 4.2 / SODIUM 568 / CHOLESTEROL 30

Italian Beef and Rice Casserole

1 lb. lean ground beef
1 cup onion, chopped
½ cup green pepper,
    chopped
½ cup celery, chopped
1 (14½ oz.) can tomatoes
1 (6 oz.) can Italian
    tomato paste
1 (4 oz.) can mushroom
    pieces, drained
2 tablespoons fresh
    parsley, snipped
1 teaspoon salt
½ teaspoon pepper
¼ teaspoon thyme
¼ teaspoon marjoram
1 cup rice, cooked
1 cup Cheddar cheese,
    shredded

In 2-quart casserole, combine ground beef, onion, green pepper and celery. Microwave at HIGH (10) 5 to 7 minutes until vegetables are tender. Drain. Add tomatoes, tomato paste, mushrooms, parsley, salt, pepper, thyme, marjoram and rice. Microwave at HIGH (10) 13 to 18 minutes. Top with Cheddar cheese and continue to Microwave at HIGH (10) 2 to 3 minutes until cheese melts. Yield: 6 servings (327 calories per serving).

Total Microwave Cooking Time 20 to 28 Minutes

PROTEIN 18.2 / FAT 18.6 / CARBOHYDRATE 22.2 / SODIUM 884 / CHOLESTEROL 62

Eggs & Cheese

Normandy Omelet

2 tablespoons butter,
   melted, divided
4 eggs, separated
Salt and pepper to taste
1 cup fresh strawberries,
   sliced
1 tablespoon honey
Powdered sugar, optional

In 9-inch pie plate, place 1 tablespoon melted butter. Turn plate to coat bottom. Set aside. In small mixing bowl, beat egg whites until stiff but not dry. In 4-cup glass measure, beat egg yolks, salt and pepper until thickened. Fold egg yolks into egg whites; carefully pour mixture into pie plate. Microwave at HIGH (10) 1 to 2 minutes. Rotate dish ¼ turn. Microwave at HIGH (10) 1 to 2 minutes. Let stand 2 minutes. With spatula, loosen edges of omelet from plate.

In small bowl, combine strawberries, honey and remaining butter. Mix well. Spoon strawberries onto half of omelet. Fold other half over strawberries. Sprinkle with powdered sugar, if desired.
Yield: 1 serving (523 calories).

Total Microwave Cooking Time 2 to 4 Minutes

PROTEIN 19.2 / FAT 37.1 / CARBOHYDRATE 30.9 / SODIUM 432 / CHOLESTEROL 707

Basic Omelet

1 tablespoon butter
3 eggs, room temperature
1 tablespoon water
⅛ teaspoon salt
Dash pepper

In 9-inch pie plate, place butter. Microwave at HIGH (10) 30 to 45 seconds until melted. Turn plate to coat. In medium mixing bowl, combine eggs, water, salt and pepper. Beat with a wire whisk until blended. Pour mixture into pie plate. Cover with plastic wrap. Microwave at HIGH (10) 1 to 2 minutes until omelet is almost set; stir after 30 seconds. Let stand, covered, 2 minutes. Using a spatula, loosen edges of omelet from plate; fold over and serve. Yield: 1 serving (382 calories).

Total Microwave Cooking Time 1½ to 2¾ Minutes

PROTEIN 22.8 / FAT 30.8 / CARBOHYDRATE 2.2 / SODIUM 581 / CHOLESTEROL 790

Vegetable Frittata

2 tablespoons butter
1 small onion, sliced
4 asparagus spears, sliced
3 fresh mushrooms, sliced
½ small zucchini, sliced
8 eggs, beaten
½ cup milk
¼ teaspoon salt
⅛ teaspoon pepper
Dash hot sauce

Place butter and onion in 9-inch quiche dish. Microwave at HIGH (10) 1 to 3 minutes. Add asparagus, mushrooms and zucchini. Microwave at HIGH (10) 3 to 5 minutes; stir after 2 minutes. In small mixing bowl, combine eggs, milk, salt, pepper and hot sauce. Pour over vegetables. Microwave at MEDIUM HIGH (7) 10 to 14 minutes. Yield: 4 servings (269 calories per serving).

Total Microwave Cooking Time 14 to 22 Minutes

PROTEIN 17.5 / FAT 19.1 / CARBOHYDRATE 6.7 / SODIUM 375 / CHOLESTEROL 536

Eggs & Cheese

▲ *Ham and Egg Casserole*

Ham and Egg Casserole

**3 cups white bread cubes,
    crusts removed**
**2 cups sharp Cheddar
    cheese, shredded**
**¼ cup green onion,
    finely chopped**
**1 (4½ oz.) jar sliced
    mushrooms, drained**
**1 cup ham, cut into
    ½-inch cubes**
4 eggs
½ cup milk
1 teaspoon dry mustard
⅛ teaspoon pepper
Dash hot sauce

In 2-quart oblong glass baking dish, place cubed bread. Sprinkle cheese, green onion and mushrooms over bread. Top with ham cubes. In small mixing bowl, beat together eggs, milk, dry mustard, pepper and hot sauce. Pour egg mixture over bread, cheese and ham. Cover with wax paper. Microwave at HIGH (10) 2 to 4 minutes. Microwave at MEDIUM (5) 6 to 9 minutes until nearly set. Let stand 5 minutes before serving. Yield: 6 servings (316 calories per serving).

Total Microwave Cooking Time 8 to 13 Minutes

PROTEIN 22.4 / FAT 20.1 / CARBOHYDRATE 10.5 / SODIUM 815 / CHOLESTEROL 229

Spinach Quiche

1 tablespoon butter
1¾ cups fresh mushrooms, sliced
1 (12 oz.) pkg. frozen spinach souffle, thawed
½ lb. sweet Italian sausage, cooked and crumbled
¾ cup Swiss cheese, shredded
2 eggs, beaten
3 tablespoons whipping cream
½ teaspoon pepper
½ teaspoon hot sauce
1 (9-inch) pie crust, baked

In 2-quart casserole, combine butter and mushrooms. Microwave at HIGH (10) 2 to 4 minutes until mushrooms are tender. Drain well. Add spinach souffle, sausage, cheese, eggs, cream, pepper and hot sauce. Pour into crust. Microwave at MEDIUM HIGH (7) 13 to 20 minutes until center is set but not dry. Let stand 5 minutes. Yield: 6 servings (450 calories per serving).

Total Microwave Cooking Time 15 to 24 Minutes

PROTEIN 17.7 / FAT 33.5 / CARBOHYDRATE 19.5 / SODIUM 803 / CHOLESTEROL 206

Garlic Cheese and Grits Casserole

3 cups hot tap water
¾ cup quick cooking grits
¾ teaspoon salt
5 tablespoons butter, sliced
1½ cups sharp Cheddar cheese, shredded
2 eggs, beaten
Milk
¼ teaspoon garlic powder
Dash hot sauce
½ cup sharp Cheddar cheese, shredded
Paprika

In 3-quart casserole, place water, grits and salt. Microwave at HIGH (10) 8 to 12 minutes; stir after 5 minutes. Add butter and 1½ cups cheese to grits. Stir well until melted. In 1-cup glass measure, beat eggs; add enough milk to total ¾ cup. Add garlic powder and hot sauce. Quickly stir into grits. Pour into well-greased 8-inch square glass baking dish. Sprinkle remaining cheese over top. Sprinkle with paprika. Microwave at MEDIUM HIGH (7) 15 to 20 minutes. Let stand 5 minutes before serving. Yield: 6 servings (346 calories per serving).

Total Microwave Cooking Time 23 to 32 Minutes

PROTEIN 14.0 / FAT 24.7 / CARBOHYDRATE 16.8 / SODIUM 655 / CHOLESTEROL 153

Swiss Cheese Fondue

4 cups Swiss cheese, shredded
¼ cup all-purpose flour
⅛ teaspoon garlic powder
⅛ teaspoon pepper
Dash nutmeg
1 cup white wine or apple juice
2 tablespoons Kirsch, optional
French bread, cut into cubes, or bread sticks

In medium mixing bowl, toss cheese with flour, garlic powder, pepper and nutmeg. In 2-quart casserole, add wine. Microwave at HIGH (10) 2 to 3 minutes. Gradually add 2 cups of cheese mixture; stir until smooth. Microwave at MEDIUM (5) 2 to 3 minutes; stir after 1 minute. Add remaining cheese mixture and Kirsch; stir until smooth. Microwave at MEDIUM (5) 2 to 3 minutes until cheese is melted; stir after 1 minute. Serve hot with French bread. Yield: 6 servings (552 calories per serving).

Total Microwave Cooking Time 6 to 9 Minutes

PROTEIN 29.0 / FAT 22.3 / CARBOHYDRATE 49.8 / SODIUM 643 / CHOLESTEROL 72

Eggs & Cheese

▲ *Cheese Enchiladas*

Cheese Enchiladas

1 (15 oz.) carton
  ricotta cheese
1 egg, beaten
1 cup green onions,
  chopped
2 tablespoons green chilies,
  chopped
1 teaspoon cumin
1 cup Monterey Jack
  cheese, shredded
8 (6-in.) corn or flour
  tortillas
1 (10 oz.) can
  enchilada sauce
2 cups Cheddar cheese,
  shredded
Sour cream, optional
Green onions, chopped,
  optional

In mixing bowl, combine ricotta cheese, egg, onions, chilies, cumin and Monterey Jack cheese.

Wrap tortillas in paper towel. Microwave at HIGH (10) ½ minute until pliable. Divide cheese mixture evenly among tortillas. Roll up tightly.

Place tortillas in 2-quart oblong glass baking dish, seam side down. Pour enchilada sauce over tortillas. Microwave at HIGH (10) 9 to 13 minutes.

Top with Cheddar cheese. Microwave at HIGH (10) 1 to 2 minutes until cheese is almost melted. Garnish with sour cream and green onions, if desired. Yield: 4 servings (678 calories per serving).

Total Microwave Cooking Time 10½ to 15½ Minutes

PROTEIN 41.5 / FAT 40.2 / CARBOHYDRATE 39.6 / SODIUM 1200 / CHOLESTEROL 181

Breakfast Cheese Pizza

3 green onions, chopped
1 tablespoon bacon
   drippings
½ cup fresh mushrooms,
   finely chopped
5 slices bread, buttered
Garlic salt
1 cup Cheddar cheese,
   shredded
1 cup Swiss cheese,
   shredded
2 tablespoons all-purpose
   flour
6 slices bacon, cooked
   and crumbled
1½ cups milk
2 eggs
¼ teaspoon salt
¼ teaspoon pepper

In 2-quart casserole, combine onions, bacon drippings and mushrooms. Microwave at HIGH (10) 2 to 3 minutes until onions are transparent and mushrooms are tender. Set aside. Sprinkle buttered bread with garlic salt. Cut slices in half diagonally. Arrange buttered side down in 10-inch pie plate, forming a crust. Sprinkle onions and mushrooms over bread.

In medium mixing bowl, combine Cheddar cheese, Swiss cheese, flour and bacon. Spread over top of onions and mushrooms. In small mixing bowl, beat together milk, eggs, salt and pepper. Pour evenly over cheese. Microwave at MEDIUM HIGH (7) 9 to 12 minutes until knife inserted in center comes out clean. Yield: 6 servings (460 calories per serving).

Arrange sliced bread buttered side down to form crust.

Total Microwave Cooking Time 11 to 15 Minutes

PROTEIN 24.6 / FAT 32.2 / CARBOHYDRATE 17.9 / SODIUM 644 / CHOLESTEROL 169

Cheese Rarebit

1 (8 oz.) pkg. pasteurized
   processed cheese, diced
1 tablespoon butter
½ teaspoon
   Worcestershire sauce
¼ teaspoon salt
¼ teaspoon dry mustard
Dash cayenne pepper
¼ cup half & half
1 egg yolk, beaten

In 1-quart casserole, place cheese and butter. Microwave at HIGH (10) 2 minutes until smooth, stirring every minute. Add Worcestershire sauce, salt, mustard and cayenne pepper. Quickly stir in half & half and egg yolk. Microwave at MEDIUM (5) 4 to 5 minutes until hot, stirring every minute. Serve over toast.
Yield: 3 servings (366 calories per serving).

Total Microwave Cooking Time 6 to 7 Minutes

PROTEIN 18.4 / FAT 31.6 / CARBOHYDRATE 2.4 / SODIUM 1334 / CHOLESTEROL 161

Southwest Scrambled Eggs

8 eggs
1 cup Cheddar cheese,
   shredded
¼ cup milk
¼ teaspoon salt
¼ teaspoon pepper
½ cup cooked ham,
   chopped
1 (4 oz.) can chopped
   green chilies, drained

In 2-quart casserole, combine eggs, cheese, milk, salt and pepper. Beat with wire whisk until well blended. Cover with plastic wrap and vent. Microwave at HIGH (10) 2 to 4 minutes. Stir. Add ham and green chilies. Microwave at HIGH (10) 3 to 5 minutes until set; stir after 3 minutes. Yield: 4 servings (349 calories per serving).

Total Microwave Cooking Time 5 to 9 Minutes

PROTEIN 27.6 / FAT 23.8 / CARBOHYDRATE 5.0 / SODIUM 776 / CHOLESTEROL 560

Sauces

Raisin Sauce

½ cup orange juice
½ cup water
1 tablespoon cornstarch
1 tablespoon rum, optional
½ cup raisins
⅓ cup currant jelly
Dash allspice

In 1½-quart casserole, stir together orange juice, water and cornstarch until blended. Stir in rum, raisins, currant jelly and allspice. Microwave at HIGH (10) 3 to 5 minutes until sauce is thickened, stirring every 2 minutes. Yield: 1½ cups (24 calories per tablespoon).

Total Microwave Cooking Time 3 to 5 Minutes

PROTEIN 0.1 / FAT 0.0 / CARBOHYDRATE 6.2 / SODIUM 1 / CHOLESTEROL 0

Barbecue Sauce

2 tablespoons butter
1 small onion, grated
1 cup catsup
⅓ cup white vinegar
¼ cup Worcestershire sauce
½ cup brown sugar, firmly packed
1 tablespoon chili powder
2 teaspoons pepper
¼ teaspoon seasoned salt
⅛ teaspoon garlic powder

In 2-quart casserole, place butter and onion. Microwave at HIGH (10) 2 to 3 minutes until onion is tender. Add catsup, vinegar, Worcestershire sauce, brown sugar, chili powder, pepper, seasoned salt and garlic powder. Cover. Microwave at HIGH (10) 5 minutes. Stir and continue to Microwave, covered, at MEDIUM HIGH (7) 7 to 10 minutes until sauce is thickened, stirring every 3 minutes. Yield: 2 cups (32 calories per tablespoon).

Total Microwave Cooking Time 14 to 18 Minutes

PROTEIN 0.3 / FAT 0.8 / CARBOHYDRATE 6.4 / SODIUM 132 / CHOLESTEROL 2

Red Clam Sauce

½ teaspoon olive oil
1 clove garlic, minced
2 (6 ½ oz.) cans minced clams
2 (8 oz.) cans tomato sauce
2 tablespoons tomato paste
2 tablespoons fresh parsley, snipped
2 tablespoons onion, chopped
2 tablespoons grated Parmesan cheese
½ teaspoon basil
½ teaspoon oregano
⅛ teaspoon freshly ground pepper

In 2-quart casserole, combine olive oil and garlic. Microwave at MEDIUM HIGH (7) 1 to 2 minutes. Drain clams, reserving juice from one can. Set clams aside.

Combine clam juice, tomato sauce, tomato paste, parsley, onion, Parmesan cheese, basil, oregano and pepper; add to casserole. Cover. Microwave at MEDIUM HIGH (7) 7 to 10 minutes. Stir in clams and Microwave at HIGH (10) 2 to 3 minutes. Serve over pasta. Yield: 3 cups (124 calories per ½ cup).

Total Microwave Cooking Time 10 to 15 Minutes

PROTEIN 17.4 / FAT 2.3 / CARBOHYDRATE 8.3 / SODIUM 390 / CHOLESTEROL 43

Sauces

▲ *Homemade Spaghetti Sauce*

Homemade Spaghetti Sauce

2 tablespoons oil
¾ cup onion, chopped
2 cloves garlic,
** finely chopped**
1 (28 oz.) can whole
** tomatoes, chopped**
1 (6 oz.) can tomato paste
½ cup water
1 bay leaf
½ teaspoon salt
¼ teaspoon basil
¼ teaspoon oregano

In 3-quart casserole, combine oil, onion and garlic. Microwave at HIGH (10) 1 to 2 minutes. Add tomatoes, tomato paste, water, bay leaf, salt, basil and oregano. Cover. Microwave at HIGH (10) 6 to 7 minutes; stir after 3 minutes. Continue to Microwave at MEDIUM (5) 1 hour, stirring every 10 minutes. Yield: 6 cups (100 calories per cup).

Meat Sauce: Add ½ pound ground beef or sausage, cooked and drained.

Total Microwave Cooking Time 1 hour 7 Minutes to 1 hour 9 Minutes

PROTEIN 2.6 / FAT 5.1 / CARBOHYDRATE 13.1 / SODIUM 430 / CHOLESTEROL 0

Lemon Butter Sauce

¼ cup butter
1 tablespoon fresh
** lemon juice**
1 tablespoon fresh
** parsley, snipped**
1 teaspoon grated
** lemon rind**
Dash lemon pepper

In 1-cup glass measure, place butter. Microwave at HIGH (10) ½ to 1 minute until melted. Stir in lemon juice, parsley, lemon rind and lemon pepper. Serve warm. Yield: ¼ cup (103 calories per tablespoon).

Total Microwave Cooking Time ½ to 1 Minute

PROTEIN 0.2 / FAT 11.5 / CARBOHYDRATE 0.4 / SODIUM 118 / CHOLESTEROL 31

Basic White Sauce

2 tablespoons butter,
  melted
2 tablespoons all-purpose
  flour
¼ teaspoon salt
1 cup milk

In 1½-quart casserole, combine melted butter, flour and salt. Gradually add milk; stir until smooth. Microwave at MEDIUM (5) 3 to 5 minutes until sauce is thickened, stirring every minute with a wire whisk. Yield: 1 cup (26 calories per tablespoon).

Cheese Sauce: Stir in ½ to ¾ cup shredded cheese. Microwave at MEDIUM (5) 1 minute, if necessary, to melt cheese completely.

Curry Sauce: Stir in 1 to 2 teaspoons curry powder.

Horseradish Sauce: Stir in 1 tablespoon prepared horseradish.

Total Microwave Cooking Time 3 to 5 Minutes

PROTEIN 0.6 / FAT 2.0 / CARBOHYDRATE 1.5 / SODIUM 59 / CHOLESTEROL 6

To make a cheese sauce, add shredded cheese to the Basic White Sauce recipe.

Mushroom Sauce

2 cups fresh mushrooms,
  sliced
¼ cup butter
¼ cup water
¼ cup dry sherry
1 tablespoon cornstarch
⅛ teaspoon salt

In 1-quart casserole, place mushrooms and butter; cover. Microwave at MEDIUM HIGH (7) 3 minutes.

Combine water, sherry, cornstarch and salt; stir until smooth. Gradually add to mushroom mixture. Microwave at HIGH (10) 2 to 4 minutes until thickened, stirring once. Yield: 2 cups (17 calories per tablespoon).

Total Microwave Cooking Time 5 to 7 Minutes

PROTEIN 0.1 / FAT 1.5 / CARBOHYDRATE 0.5 / SODIUM 24 / CHOLESTEROL 4

Sweet and Sour Sauce

½ cup sugar
2 tablespoons cornstarch
¼ cup water
1 (8 oz.) can crushed
  pineapple
½ cup green pepper,
  chopped
1 (4 oz.) jar sliced pimento
1 clove garlic, minced
½ cup cider vinegar
2 tablespoons soy sauce
¼ teaspoon hot sauce

In 1½-quart casserole, combine sugar, cornstarch and water. Stir in pineapple, green pepper, pimento, garlic, vinegar, soy sauce and hot sauce. Microwave at HIGH (10) 3 to 5 minutes until clear and thickened, stirring every 2 minutes. Yield: 1¾ cups (24 calories per tablespoon).

Total Microwave Cooking Time 3 to 5 Minutes

PROTEIN 0.2 / FAT 0.0 / CARBOHYDRATE 6.0 / SODIUM 60 / CHOLESTEROL 0

Sauces

▲ *Vanilla Sauce*

Vanilla Sauce

⅓ cup sugar
1½ tablespoons cornstarch
1 cup milk
1 tablespoon butter
1 teaspoon vanilla

In 1-quart casserole, combine sugar and cornstarch. Add milk, stirring with a wire whisk until smooth. Microwave at HIGH (10) 3 to 4 minutes until sauce is thickened, stirring every minute with a wire whisk. Blend in butter and vanilla. Refrigerate for 30 minutes. Yield: 1½ cups (24 calories per tablespoon).

Total Microwave Cooking Time 3 to 4 Minutes

PROTEIN 0.3 / FAT 0.8 / CARBOHYDRATE 3.8 / SODIUM 10 / CHOLESTEROL 3

To flame, carefully ignite warmed brandy in spoon and pour over fruit.

Brandied Cherry Sauce

1 (17 oz.) can dark sweet pitted cherries in heavy syrup
½ cup sugar
1½ tablespoons cornstarch
1 cup water
¼ cup brandy

Drain cherries, reserving ¼ cup syrup. In 1-quart casserole, combine sugar and cornstarch. Add cherries, syrup and water, stirring until smooth. Microwave at HIGH (10) 3 to 4 minutes until sauce is thickened, stirring every minute. Spoon sauce over dessert. Microwave brandy in 1-cup glass measure at HIGH (10) 30 to 45 seconds. Remove one tablespoon brandy into metal spoon. Pour remaining brandy over cherries. Ignite brandy in spoon and pour over cherries to flame. Yield: 1½ cups (40 calories per tablespoon).

Total Microwave Cooking Time 3½ to 4¾ Minutes

PROTEIN 0.1 / FAT 0.0 / CARBOHYDRATE 8.9 / SODIUM 1 / CHOLESTEROL 0

Rich Butterscotch Sauce

1¼ cups brown sugar,
   firmly packed
1 tablespoon cornstarch
½ cup half & half
2 tablespoons light corn
   syrup
⅛ teaspoon salt
¼ cup butter
1 teaspoon vanilla

In 1½-quart casserole, combine brown sugar and cornstarch. Stir in half & half, corn syrup and salt; add butter. Microwave at HIGH (10) 2 to 5 minutes until thickened and sugar is dissolved, stirring once. Add vanilla; blend well. Serve warm or cold. Yield: 1½ cups (57 calories per tablespoon).

Total Microwave Cooking Time 2 to 5 Minutes

PROTEIN 0.2 / FAT 0.6 / CARBOHYDRATE 12.9 / SODIUM 19 / CHOLESTEROL 2

Hot Fudge Sauce

1 cup (6 oz.) semi-sweet
   chocolate pieces
½ cup light corn syrup
¼ cup milk
1 tablespoon butter
1 teaspoon vanilla

In 1½-quart casserole, combine chocolate and syrup. Microwave at MEDIUM HIGH (7) 4 to 6 minutes, stirring every 2 minutes. Gradually add milk; stir until smooth. Blend in butter and vanilla. Yield: 1½ cups (60 calories per tablespoon).

Total Microwave Cooking Time 4 to 6 Minutes

PROTEIN 0.5 / FAT 2.8 / CARBOHYDRATE 9.5 / SODIUM 11 / CHOLESTEROL 2

Crunchy Chocolate Sauce

¼ cup milk
1 (1 oz.) square
   unsweetened chocolate
¾ cup brown sugar,
   firmly packed
¼ cup crunchy
   peanut butter
¼ teaspoon vanilla

In 2-cup glass measure, combine milk and chocolate. Microwave at HIGH (10) 1 to 2 minutes. Stir to blend well. Add sugar; stir. Microwave at HIGH (10) 1 to 2 minutes until mixture boils. Add peanut butter and vanilla; stir thoroughly. Serve warm or cool. Yield: 1 cup (74 calories per tablespoon).

Total Microwave Cooking Time 2 to 4 Minutes

PROTEIN 1.3 / FAT 3.1 / CARBOHYDRATE 11.5 / SODIUM 25 / CHOLESTEROL 1

Hawaiian Strawberry Sauce

1 (10 oz.) pkg. frozen sliced
   strawberries, thawed
½ cup currant jelly
2 tablespoons cornstarch
2 tablespoons pineapple
   juice

In 1½-quart casserole, place strawberries and jelly; cover. Microwave at HIGH (10) 2 to 4 minutes until mixture boils.

Combine cornstarch and pineapple juice; add to strawberry mixture. Microwave at HIGH (10) 1 to 3 minutes until thickened, stirring once. Yield: 1½ cups (32 calories per tablespoon).

Total Microwave Cooking Time 3 to 7 Minutes

PROTEIN 0.1 / FAT 0.0 / CARBOHYDRATE 8.2 / SODIUM 1 / CHOLESTEROL 0

Vegetables

Acorn Squash with Cranberry Filling

2 medium acorn squash
  (about 2 lbs.)
1 (16 oz.) can whole berry
  cranberry sauce
1 tablespoon honey
¼ teaspoon allspice

Prick squash several times with fork to allow steam to escape. Place in oven. Microwave at HIGH (10) 13 to 22 minutes until soft when pricked with fork. Turn squash over and rearrange after 9 minutes. Let stand 5 minutes. Cut in half and remove seeds. Place cut side up in 10-inch pie plate.

In small bowl, combine cranberry sauce, honey and allspice. Microwave at HIGH (10) 3 to 5 minutes until hot and bubbly; stir after 2 minutes. Spoon into squash halves. Microwave at HIGH (10) 3 to 4 minutes until heated through. Yield: 4 servings (267 calories per serving).

Total Microwave Cooking Time 19 to 31 Minutes

PROTEIN 1.8 / FAT 0.4 / CARBOHYDRATE 69.2 / SODIUM 39 / CHOLESTEROL 0

Stir-Fry Vegetables

1 tablespoon oil
2 tablespoons soy sauce
1 tablespoon butter
¼ teaspoon garlic powder
3 medium onions,
  quartered lengthwise
2 cups cabbage,
  thinly sliced
1 medium green pepper,
  cut in ¼-inch strips
1 cup broccoli flowerets
1 cup cauliflower flowerets
⅔ cup carrots, sliced
  diagonally
2 stalks celery,
  sliced diagonally
¼ cup green onions, sliced

In 3-quart casserole, place oil, soy sauce, butter and garlic powder. Microwave at HIGH (10) ½ to 1 minute until hot. Add onions, cabbage, green pepper, broccoli, cauliflower, carrots, celery, and green onions. Toss to coat. Cover. Microwave at HIGH (10) 9 to 15 minutes; stir after 6 minutes. Serve immediately. Yield: 8 servings (72 calories per serving).

Total Microwave Cooking Time 9½ to 16 Minutes

PROTEIN 2.1 / FAT 3.4 / CARBOHYDRATE 9.7 / SODIUM 246 / CHOLESTEROL 4

Zesty Tomatoes & Squash

¼ cup butter, melted
1 teaspoon oregano
½ teaspoon basil
½ teaspoon seasoned salt
⅛ teaspoon garlic powder
⅛ teaspoon pepper
2 medium zucchini,
  thinly sliced
1 medium yellow squash,
  thinly sliced
2 small tomatoes, each cut
  into 4 wedges

In 2-quart casserole, combine butter, oregano, basil, seasoned salt and pepper. Add zucchini and yellow squash. Toss to coat. Cover. Microwave at HIGH (10) 6 to 10 minutes until vegetables are tender; stir after 3 minutes. Add tomatoes. Cover; let stand 2 minutes. Yield: 4 servings (141 calories per serving).

Total Microwave Cooking Time 6 to 10 Minutes

PROTEIN 2.3 / FAT 12.0 / CARBOHYDRATE 8.5 / SODIUM 346 / CHOLESTEROL 31

◄ *Acorn Squash with Cranberry Filling*

Vegetables

▲ *Asparagus with Mustard Dressing*

Arrange with tips to the center of dish.

Asparagus with Mustard Dressing

½ cup mayonnaise
2 tablespoons onion, finely chopped
1 tablespoon white wine
2 teaspoons prepared mustard
½ teaspoon soy sauce
⅛ teaspoon ginger
⅛ teaspoon white pepper
1 lb. fresh asparagus
¼ cup water

In 2-cup glass measure, combine mayonnaise, onion, wine, mustard, soy sauce, ginger and pepper. Mix well and refrigerate.

Arrange asparagus in 2-quart oblong glass baking dish with stalks to outside edges of dish and tips to center. Add water; cover with plastic wrap, turning back one corner to vent. Microwave at HIGH (10) 1 to 3 minutes until crisp-tender. Drain and chill.

Arrange asparagus spears on serving platter. Top with mustard dressing. Yield: 3 servings (294 calories per serving).

Total Microwave Cooking Time 1 to 3 Minutes

PROTEIN 3.6 / FAT 29.5 / CARBOHYDRATE 5.7 / SODIUM 301 / CHOLESTEROL 22

Pecan Crisp Squash

⅔ cup buttery cracker
    crumbs
⅓ cup pecans, chopped
⅓ cup butter, melted
3 tablespoons brown sugar
½ teaspoon salt
¼ teaspoon nutmeg
2 acorn squash
    (about 1 lb. each)

Combine crumbs, pecans, butter, brown sugar, salt and nutmeg; set aside.

Cut squash in half lengthwise; remove seeds. Place squash, cut side down, in 2-quart oblong glass baking dish. Cover with vented plastic wrap. Microwave at HIGH (10) 4 to 6 minutes. Turn squash cut side up. Divide filling evenly among squash halves. Recover. Microwave at HIGH (10) 4 to 8 minutes until tender. Let stand, uncovered, 5 minutes. Yield: 4 servings (371 calories per serving).

Total Microwave Cooking Time 8 to 14 Minutes

PROTEIN 2.5 / FAT 25.7 / CARBOHYDRATE 36.9 / SODIUM 585 / CHOLESTEROL 41

Corn Pudding

1 (16 oz.) can whole kernel
    corn
3 eggs, beaten
1 cup milk
2 tablespoons butter,
    melted
2 tablespoons all-purpose
    flour
2 tablespoons sugar
½ teaspoon salt

In 1½-quart casserole, combine corn, eggs, milk, butter, flour, sugar and salt. Microwave at HIGH (10) 11 to 16 minutes until center is barely set. Let stand 5 minutes. Yield: 4 servings (284 calories per serving).

Total Microwave Cooking Time 11 to 16 Minutes

PROTEIN 10.9 / FAT 13.0 / CARBOHYDRATE 34.6 / SODIUM 442 / CHOLESTEROL 218

Cheesy Broccoli

1 (10 oz.) pkg. frozen
    chopped broccoli
1 cup instant rice
1 (10 ¾ oz.) can cream of
    chicken soup
1 (8 oz.) jar processed
    cheese spread
½ cup milk
½ teaspoon salt
¼ teaspoon pepper
½ cup celery, chopped
¼ cup onion, chopped

Place broccoli in 2-quart casserole. Cover. Microwave at HIGH (10) 4 to 7 minutes; drain. Set aside.

In 2-quart casserole, combine rice, soup, cheese, milk, salt and pepper. Microwave at HIGH (10) 2 to 4 minutes until cheese melts and can be blended easily.

To cheese mixture, add celery, onion and broccoli. Stir thoroughly. Cover. Microwave at MEDIUM HIGH (7) 11 to 18 minutes. Remove cover for last 2 to 3 minutes of cooking time. Let stand 5 minutes. Yield: 6 servings (309 calories per serving).

Total Microwave Cooking Time 17 to 29 Minutes

PROTEIN 12.4 / FAT 12.2 / CARBOHYDRATE 38.6 / SODIUM 1137 / CHOLESTEROL 28

Vegetables

▲ *Stuffed Yellow Squash*

Scoop out pulp and seeds leaving ¼-inch thick shell.

Stuffed Yellow Squash

3 large yellow squash
¼ lb. hot bulk sausage
½ cup green pepper, chopped
¼ cup onion, chopped
1 medium tomato, chopped
½ cup grated Parmesan cheese
1 cup mozzarella cheese, shredded

Cut squash in half lengthwise. Scoop out pulp and seeds and discard, leaving ¼-inch thick shell. Set aside. In 2-quart casserole, combine sausage, green pepper and onion. Cover. Microwave at MEDIUM HIGH (7) 3 to 5 minutes until sausage is brown; stir every 2 minutes. Drain. Add tomato and Parmesan cheese. Stir until well blended.

Spoon mixture into squash shells; place squash in 2-quart oblong glass baking dish. Cover with wax paper. Microwave at HIGH (10) 13 to 18 minutes; rotate dish ½ turn after 8 minutes. Sprinkle with mozzarella cheese. Microwave at HIGH (10) 1 to 3 minutes until cheese is melted. Yield: 6 servings (166 calories per serving).

Total Microwave Cooking Time 17 to 26 Minutes

PROTEIN 10.9 / FAT 9.5 / CARBOHYDRATE 11.2 / SODIUM 323 / CHOLESTEROL 28

Delicious Yams

1 (30 oz.) can yams,
   well drained
⅓ cup orange juice
1 tablespoon cornstarch
½ cup brown sugar,
   firmly packed
¼ cup butter, melted
½ cup walnuts,
   coarsely chopped
1½ cups miniature
   marshmallows

Arrange yams in 1½-quart casserole. In medium bowl, combine orange juice and cornstarch; stir until cornstarch is completely dissolved. Blend in brown sugar and butter. Add walnuts and pour over yams. Microwave at HIGH (10) 6 to 10 minutes. Arrange marshmallows on top and Microwave at HIGH (10) 1 to 2 minutes. Yield: 4 servings (549 calories per serving).

Total Microwave Cooking Time 9 to 14 Minutes

PROTEIN 4.6 / FAT 21.2 / CARBOHYDRATE 89.0 / SODIUM 217 / CHOLESTEROL 31

Scalloped Potatoes

3 tablespoons butter
2 tablespoons all-purpose
   flour
1 teaspoon salt
¼ teaspoon pepper
3 cups milk
4 cups potatoes,
   peeled and thinly sliced
   (about 2 lbs.)
¼ cup onion,
   finely chopped
Paprika

In 4-cup glass measure, place butter. Microwave at HIGH (10) ½ to 1 minute until melted. Blend in flour, salt and pepper. Gradually add milk, stirring until smooth. Microwave at HIGH (10) 6 to 10 minutes until sauce is smooth and slightly thickened, stirring every 3 minutes. In 2-quart casserole, layer half of potatoes, onions and sauce. Repeat layers. Cover. Microwave at HIGH (10) 14 to 20 minutes until potatoes are tender. Sprinkle with paprika. Let stand, covered, 5 minutes. Yield: 6 servings (257 calories per serving).

Total Microwave Cooking Time 20½ to 31 Minutes

PROTEIN 7.5 / FAT 10.0 / CARBOHYDRATE 35.5 / SODIUM 518 / CHOLESTEROL 33

Potato-Cheese Hurry-Up

1 (10½ oz.) can cream of
   celery soup
½ cup onion, chopped
½ cup Cheddar cheese,
   shredded
¼ teaspoon dillweed
¼ teaspoon salt
¼ teaspoon pepper
2 (16 oz.) cans sliced
   potatoes, drained
2 tablespoons grated
   Parmesan cheese

In 1½-quart casserole, combine soup, onion, Cheddar cheese, dillweed, salt and pepper. Add potatoes and mix thoroughly; cover. Microwave at HIGH (10) 7 to 11 minutes until hot, stirring after 5 minutes. Sprinkle with Parmesan cheese before serving. Yield: 4 servings (173 calories per serving).

Total Microwave Cooking Time 7 to 11 Minutes

PROTEIN 7.2 / FAT 8.9 / CARBOHYDRATE 16.6 / SODIUM 1165 / CHOLESTEROL 25

Vegetables

▲ *Wilted Spinach Salad*

Wilted Spinach Salad

3 strips bacon
¼ cup vinegar
2 teaspoons sugar
¼ teaspoon salt
⅛ teaspoon pepper
⅛ teaspoon tarragon
½ cup celery, sliced
1 small red onion,
  thinly sliced
1 pkg. fresh spinach leaves,
  torn (about 8 cups total)
2 medium oranges, peeled
  and sliced*
⅓ cup cashews,
  coarsely broken

Snip bacon into 1-inch pieces and place in 3-quart casserole. Cover with paper towel. Microwave at HIGH (10) 1 to 3 minutes until crisp. With slotted spoon, place bacon on paper towels to drain.

To bacon drippings add vinegar, sugar, salt, pepper and tarragon. Microwave at HIGH (10) 1 to 3 minutes until mixture boils. Stir in celery and onion.

Gradually add spinach to hot dressing, tossing to coat evenly. Add crumbled bacon, orange segments and cashews. Toss again lightly. Serve immediately. Yield: 8 servings (87 calories per serving).

*If desired, substitute 1 (11 oz.) can Mandarin oranges, drained.

Total Microwave Cooking Time 2 to 6 Minutes

PROTEIN 3.8 / FAT 4.3 / CARBOHYDRATE 10.4 / SODIUM 206 / CHOLESTEROL 2

Sweet & Sour Beets

1 lb. fresh beets
1 cup water
3 tablespoons sugar
2 tablespoons butter,
   melted
2 tablespoons cider
   vinegar

Wash beets; remove tops. In 2-quart casserole, place beets and water. Cover. Microwave at HIGH (10) 8 to 12 minutes until tender; stir after 5 minutes. Drain and cool. Peel beets and cut into quarters. Return beets to casserole. Add sugar, butter and vinegar; cover. Microwave at HIGH (10) 3 to 5 minutes; stir after 2 minutes. Yield: 4 servings (116 calories per serving).

Total Microwave Cooking Time 11 to 17 Minutes

PROTEIN 1.0 / FAT 6.2 / CARBOHYDRATE 15.8 / SODIUM 103 / CHOLESTEROL 16

Company Cauliflower

2 (10 oz.) pkgs. frozen
   cauliflower
2 tablespoons water
1½ tablespoons olive oil
1 tablespoon all-purpose
   flour
1 cup small-curd
   cottage cheese
½ cup Cheddar cheese,
   shredded
½ cup milk
1 (2 oz.) jar sliced pimento,
   drained
½ teaspoon salt
⅛ teaspoon pepper
½ cup cornflakes, crushed
½ teaspoon paprika
½ teaspoon dillweed

In 2-quart casserole, place cauliflower and water; cover. Microwave at HIGH (10) 5 to 7 minutes until tender. Drain and set cauliflower aside. In same casserole, combine oil and flour; stir in cheeses, milk, pimento, salt and pepper. Microwave at HIGH (10) 3 to 4 minutes until mixture thickens and cheese melts. Stir after 2 minutes. Add cauliflower; stir well. Combine cornflakes, paprika and dillweed; sprinkle over cauliflower. Microwave at HIGH (10) 3 to 5 minutes until hot. Yield: 6 servings (123 calories per serving).

Total Microwave Cooking Time 11 to 16 Minutes

PROTEIN 8.8 / FAT 6.8 / CARBOHYDRATE 7.0 / SODIUM 449 / CHOLESTEROL 18

Eggplant Italiano

1 medium eggplant
2 (8 oz.) cans tomato sauce
1 teaspoon oregano,
   divided
½ cup sharp Cheddar
   cheese, shredded,
   divided
1 cup mozzarella cheese,
   shredded

Peel eggplant; slice ⅛-inch thick. In bottom of 2-quart casserole, spread 2 tablespoons tomato sauce. Layer half of eggplant slices, 1 can tomato sauce, half of oregano and half of Cheddar cheese. Repeat layers; cover. Microwave at HIGH (10) 11 to 16 minutes until eggplant is tender. Add mozzarella cheese. Microwave at HIGH (10) 1 to 2 minutes until melted. Yield: 6 servings (130 calories per serving).

Total Microwave Cooking Time 12 to 18 Minutes

PROTEIN 7.7 / FAT 7.4 / CARBOHYDRATE 9.9 / SODIUM 589 / CHOLESTEROL 25

Vegetables

▲ *Hot Bean Salad*

Hot Bean Salad

4 strips bacon, cut in
  ½-inch pieces
½ cup sugar
1 tablespoon cornstarch
⅔ cup vinegar
¼ teaspoon salt
¼ teaspoon pepper
1 (16 oz.) can cut
  green beans, drained
1 (16 oz.) can cut
  wax beans, drained
1 (15 oz.) can red kidney
  beans, drained
1 medium onion, sliced

In 2-quart casserole, place bacon pieces. Microwave at HIGH (10) 2 to 4 minutes until crisp. Remove bacon from dish with slotted spoon. Drain.

To bacon drippings in casserole, add sugar and cornstarch; blend well. Stir in vinegar, salt and pepper. Microwave at HIGH (10) 2 to 4 minutes until thickened. Add beans and onion; stir to combine. Cover. Microwave at HIGH (10) 4 to 6 minutes until hot. Let stand 10 minutes. Sprinkle with bacon. Yield: 6 servings (229 calories per serving).

Total Microwave Cooking Time 8 to 14 Minutes

PROTEIN 9.6 / FAT 3.0 / CARBOHYDRATE 44.1 / SODIUM 371 / CHOLESTEROL 4

Savory Onions

3 large onions
1 tablespoon steak sauce
1 tablespoon
  Worcestershire sauce
1 tablespoon butter, melted
1 teaspoon grated
  Parmesan cheese
¼ teaspoon garlic salt
Dash hot sauce

Cut onions in half and place in 2-quart casserole. Combine remaining ingredients; brush over onion halves. Cover. Microwave at HIGH (10) 9 to 13 minutes until tender. Yield: 6 servings (56 calories per serving).

Total Microwave Cooking Time 9 to 13 Minutes

PROTEIN 1.2 / FAT 2.1 / CARBOHYDRATE 8.2 / SODIUM 164 / CHOLESTEROL 5

Favorite Green Bean Casserole

3 (9 oz.) pkgs. frozen
  French-cut green beans,
  thawed
1 (10 ¾ oz.) can cream of
  mushroom soup
1 (8 oz.) can sliced water
  chestnuts, drained
½ cup milk
1 (2 oz.) jar sliced pimento,
  drained
1 (3 oz.) can French-fried
  onions

In 2-quart casserole, combine beans, soup, water chestnuts, milk and pimento. Arrange onions around edge of dish. Cover. Microwave at HIGH (10) 8 to 12 minutes until hot and bubbly. Let stand 5 minutes. Yield: 8 servings (160 calories per serving).

Total Microwave Cooking Time 8 to 12 Minutes

PROTEIN 3.6 / FAT 9.1 / CARBOHYDRATE 17.9 / SODIUM 373 / CHOLESTEROL 3

Glazed Carrots

1 lb. carrots, sliced
  ½-inch thick
¼ cup brown sugar,
  firmly packed
2 tablespoons butter
2 tablespoons water
1½ teaspoons cornstarch
¼ cup pecans, chopped

In 1-quart casserole, place carrots, brown sugar and butter; cover. Microwave at HIGH (10) 7 to 11 minutes until tender, stirring after 5 minutes.

Combine water and cornstarch; stir into carrot mixture. Add pecans. Microwave at HIGH (10) 2 to 3 minutes until thickened. Stir before serving. Yield: 4 servings (185 calories per serving).

Total Microwave Cooking Time 9 to 15 Minutes

PROTEIN 1.4 / FAT 10.5 / CARBOHYDRATE 23.5 / SODIUM 91 / CHOLESTEROL 16

Cabbage Patch Casserole

1 medium head cabbage,
  chopped
2 tablespoons water
½ teaspoon salt
4 strips bacon, cooked and
  crumbled
1 (10 ¾ oz.) can Cheddar
  cheese soup
½ cup milk
1 (3 oz.) can French-fried
  onions

In 2-quart casserole, place cabbage, water and salt; cover. Microwave at HIGH (10) 6 to 8 minutes; stir after 5 minutes. Drain. Combine crumbled bacon, soup and milk; pour over cabbage and blend well; cover. Microwave at HIGH (10) 4 to 6 minutes; stir. Sprinkle with onions. Microwave, uncovered, at HIGH (10) 1 to 2 minutes until bubbly. Yield: 6 servings (205 calories per serving).

Total Microwave Cooking Time 11 to 16 Minutes

PROTEIN 5.8 / FAT 14.7 / CARBOHYDRATE 13.4 / SODIUM 550 / CHOLESTEROL 19

Vegetable Microwaving Guide

1. Salt vegetables after cooking to avoid browning and dehydration of vegetable surface.
2. Arrange vegetables such as asparagus, with the thickest pieces to the outside edges of the dish.
3. Use casserole lid to cover vegetables when cooking. When using plastic wrap, turn back corner to vent.
4. Size of vegetable pieces affects cooking time. Larger pieces take longer.
5. For more even heating, stir vegetables during cooking.

VEGETABLE		Amount	Procedure/Comments	Power Level	Time, Minutes
Artichokes	**Fresh**	4 medium	In 3-quart casserole, place 1 cup water.	High (10)	13 to 18
Asparagus	**Fresh Cuts**	1 lb. (3 cups, cut into 1 to 2-inch pieces)	In 2-quart casserole, place ¼ cup water.	High (10)	6 to 10
	Spears	1-lb.	In 1½-quart oblong glass baking dish, place ¼ cup water.	Medium High (7)	6 to 10
	Frozen Spears	10-oz. pkg.	In 1-qt. casserole.	High (10)	5 to 7
Beans	**Fresh Green**	1 lb., cut in half	In 1½-quart casserole, place ½ cup water.	High (10)	12 to 17
	Frozen Green	10-oz. pkg.	In 1-quart casserole, place 2 tablespoons water.	High (10)	5 to 8
	Frozen Lima	10-oz. pkg.	In 1-quart casserole, place ¼ cup water.	High (10)	5 to 8
Beets	**Fresh Whole**	1 bunch	In 2-quart casserole, place ½ cup water.	High (10)	15 to 20
Broccoli	**Fresh Spears**	1 bunch (1¼ to 1½ lbs.)	In 2-quart oblong glass baking dish, place ¼ cup water.	High (10)	8 to 12
	Cut	1 bunch (1¼ to 1½ lbs.)	In 2-quart casserole, place ½ cup water.	High (10)	7 to 10
	Frozen Chopped	10-oz. pkg.	In 1-quart casserole.	High (10)	5 to 8
	Spears	10-oz. pkg.	In 1-quart casserole, place 3 tablespoons water.	High (10)	5 to 8
Brussels Sprouts	**Fresh**	1 lb.	In 1½-quart casserole, place ¼ cup water.	High (10)	7 to 10
	Frozen	10-oz. pkg.	In 1-quart casserole, place 2 tablespoons water.	High (10)	5 to 8
Cabbage	**Fresh**	1 medium head (about 2-lbs.)	In 1½ or 2-quart casserole, place ¼ cup water.	High (10)	8 to 11
	Wedges		In 2 or 3-quart casserole, place ¼ cup water.	High (10)	7 to 10
Carrots	**Fresh Sliced**	1 lb.	In 1½-quart casserole, place ¼ cup water.	High (10)	6 to 9
	Frozen	10-oz. pkg.	In 1-quart casserole, place 2 tablespoons water.	High (10)	5 to 8
Cauliflower	**Fresh Whole**	1 medium head	In 2-quart casserole, place ½ cup water.	High (10)	10 to 17
	Flowerets	1 medium head	In 2-quart casserole, place ½ cup water.	High (10)	9 to 14
	Frozen	10-oz. pkg.	In 1-quart casserole, place 2 tablespoons water.	High (10)	5 to 8

VEGETABLE		Amount	Procedure/Comments	Power Level	Time, Minutes
Corn	**Frozen Kernel**	10-oz. pkg.	In 1-quart casserole, place 2 tablespoons water.	High (10)	5 to 8
Corn on the Cob	**Fresh**	1 to 5 ears	In 2-quart oblong glass baking dish, place corn. If corn is in husk, use no water; if corn has been husked, add ¼ cup water. Rearrange after half of time.	High (10)	3 to 4 per ear
	Frozen	1 ear	In 2-quart oblong glass baking dish.	High (10)	3
		2 to 6 ears	Rearrange after half of time.	High (10)	3 to 4 per ear
Eggplant	**Fresh**	1 medium (about 1 lb.)	In 2-quart casserole, place 3 tablespoons water. Add peeled and diced eggplant.	High (10)	5 to 8
Okra	**Frozen**	10-oz. pkg.	In 1-quart casserole, place 2 tablespoons water.	High (10)	5 to 8
Parsnips	**Fresh**	1 lb.	In 1½-quart casserole, place ¼ cup water. Slice parsnips ¼-inch thick.	High (10)	7 to 10
Peas	**Fresh Shelled**	2 lbs. unshelled	In 1-quart casserole, place ¼ cup water.	High (10)	9 to 12
	Frozen	10-oz. pkg.	In 1-quart casserole, place 2 tablespoons water.	High (10)	5 to 8
Potatoes	**Fresh Whole Sweet or White**	1 (6 to 8 oz. each)	Pierce with fork. Place on paper towel on floor of microwave oven, 1-inch apart in circular arrangement. Let stand 5 minutes.	High (10)	3 to 5
		4		High (10)	15 to 17
	Fresh Cubed White	4 potatoes (6 to 8 oz. each)	Peel, cut into 1-inch cubes. Place in 2-quart casserole with ½ cup water. Stir after half of time.	High (10)	10 to 14
Spinach	**Fresh**	10 to 16 oz.	In 2-quart casserole, place washed spinach.	High (10)	5 to 8
	Frozen Chopped and Leaf	10-oz. pkg.	In 1-quart casserole, place 3 tablespoons water.	High (10)	5 to 8
Squash	**Fresh Summer and Yellow**	1 lb. sliced	In 1½-quart casserole, place ¼ cup water.	High (10)	5 to 7
	Winter Acorn or Butternut	1 to 2 squash (about 1 lb. each)	Cut in half and remove fibrous membranes. In 2-quart oblong glass baking dish, place squash cut side down. Cover with plastic wrap. Turn cut side up after half time.	High (10)	9 to 12
Succotash	**Frozen**	10-oz. pkg.	In 1-quart casserole, place 2 tablespoons water.	High (10)	5 to 8
Turnips	**Fresh**	1 lb. cubed	In 1½-quart casserole, place 3 tablespoons water.	High (10)	6 to 9
Vegetables, Mixed	**Frozen**	10-oz. pkg.	In 1-quart casserole, place 3 tablespoons water.	High (10)	5 to 8

Pastas, Cereals & Grains

Garden Pasta

3 tablespoons butter
¼ cup onion,
   finely chopped
1 clove garlic, minced
3 tablespoons all-purpose
   flour
1 teaspoon salt
¼ teaspoon thyme
2 cups milk
6 slices pasteurized
   American cheese,
   cut into pieces
1 (10 oz.) pkg. frozen
   chopped broccoli,
   thawed and well drained
½ lb. carrots, cut julienne
½ lb. zucchini, sliced
½ lb. fresh mushrooms,
   sliced
1 (7 oz.) pkg. fettuccine,
   cooked and drained

In 3-quart casserole, combine butter, onion and garlic. Microwave at HIGH (10) 1 to 3 minutes until onion is transparent. Stir in flour, salt and thyme. Gradually stir in milk. Microwave at HIGH (10) 3 to 5 minutes until thickened, stirring every 2 minutes. Blend in cheese, stirring until melted. Set aside.

In 2-quart casserole, combine broccoli, carrots, zucchini and mushrooms. Microwave at HIGH (10) 5 to 9 minutes until vegetables are tender; stir after 3 minutes. Add vegetables to cheese sauce. Mix well. Serve over fettuccine. Yield: 6 servings (388 calories per serving).

Total Microwave Cooking Time 9 to 17 Minutes

PROTEIN 16.6 / FAT 18.3 / CARBOHYDRATE 41.3 / SODIUM 926 / CHOLESTEROL 54

Deluxe Rice

2 tablespoons butter
1 cup onion, chopped
1½ cups instant rice
1½ cups water
½ teaspoon salt
1 (10 oz.) pkg. frozen
   chopped spinach,
   thawed and drained
1 cup Colby cheese,
   shredded
1 (10 ¾ oz.) can cream of
   mushroom soup
¼ teaspoon hot sauce

In 2-quart casserole, combine butter and onion. Microwave at HIGH (10) 2 to 3 minutes until onion is transparent. Add rice, water and salt. Cover. Microwave at HIGH (10) 2 to 4 minutes. Let stand, covered, 5 minutes. Add spinach, cheese, soup and hot sauce. Mix well. Microwave at MEDIUM (5) 4 to 7 minutes until heated through; stir after 3 minutes. Let stand, covered, 5 minutes before serving. Yield: 6 servings (317 calories per serving).

Total Microwave Cooking Time 8 to 14 Minutes

PROTEIN 9.9 / FAT 14.2 / CARBOHYDRATE 37.8 / SODIUM 1194 / CHOLESTEROL 29

Noodles Alfredo

1 cup grated Parmesan
   cheese
½ cup butter, sliced
½ cup whipping cream
1 tablespoon fresh parsley,
   snipped
3 cups egg noodles, cooked

In 1-quart casserole, combine Parmesan cheese, butter, whipping cream and parsley. Microwave at HIGH (10) 1½ to 3 minutes until butter melts, stirring every minute.

Add noodles. Stir to coat. Microwave at MEDIUM HIGH (7) 1½ to 3 minutes until heated through. Yield: 6 servings (371 calories per serving).

Total Microwave Cooking Time 3 to 6 Minutes

PROTEIN 9.9 | FAT 27.9 | CARBOHYDRATE 21.0 | SODIUM 418 | CHOLESTEROL 106

◄ Garden Pasta

Pastas, Cereals & Grains

▲ *Cheese Stuffed Manicotti*

Stuff cooked manicotti with cheese filling.

Cheese Stuffed Manicotti

1 cup mozzarella cheese, shredded
1 (15 oz.) carton ricotta cheese
½ cup Romano cheese
1 (7¾ oz.) can spinach, drained
½ teaspoon garlic powder
½ teaspoon salt
¼ teaspoon pepper
8 manicotti, cooked
1 (15 oz.) can tomato sauce
¼ teaspoon basil
¼ teaspoon oregano
1 cup mozzarella cheese, shredded

In medium mixing bowl, combine 1 cup mozzarella, ricotta, Romano, spinach, garlic powder, salt and pepper. Stuff cooked manicotti with cheese filling. Arrange in 2-quart oblong glass baking dish. Set aside. In 2-cup glass measure, combine tomato sauce, basil and oregano. Pour over manicotti. Sprinkle with remaining mozzarella. Cover with wax paper. Microwave at HIGH (10) 11 to 17 minutes until hot. Yield: 5 servings (496 calories per serving).

Total Microwave Cooking Time 11 to 17 Minutes

PROTEIN 30.1 / FAT 26.8 / CARBOHYDRATE 34.9 / SODIUM 1163 / CHOLESTEROL 99

Hoppin' John

1 lb. bulk pork sausage
½ cup onion, chopped
1 (15 oz.) can black-eyed peas, rinsed and drained
1 cup instant rice
3 cups hot water
½ teaspoon salt
¼ teaspoon cayenne pepper

In 3-quart casserole, place sausage and onion. Microwave at HIGH (10) 6 to 10 minutes until sausage is thoroughly cooked; stir after 4 minutes to break sausage apart; drain. Add black-eyed peas, rice, water, salt and pepper. Cover. Microwave at HIGH (10) 7 to 14 minutes until rice is cooked and most of the liquid is absorbed; stir after 5 minutes. Let stand 5 minutes before serving. Yield: 6 servings (280 calories per serving).

Total Microwave Cooking Time 13 to 24 Minutes

PROTEIN 12.4 / FAT 11.7 / CARBOHYDRATE 30.5 / SODIUM 1129 / CHOLESTEROL 29

Savory Tomato Rice

2 cups hot tap water
1 (14 ½ oz.) can tomatoes,
   cut up
1 cup long grain
   white rice
½ cup chili sauce
¼ cup green pepper,
   finely chopped
4 strips bacon, cooked
   and crumbled
2 tablespoons instant
   minced onion
1 teaspoon brown sugar
1 teaspoon salt
⅛ teaspoon pepper
½ teaspoon
   Worcestershire sauce

In 2-quart casserole, place water, tomatoes, rice, chili sauce, green pepper, bacon, onion, brown sugar, salt, pepper, water and Worcestershire sauce. Mix well. Cover. Microwave at HIGH (10) 16 to 23 minutes until hot and rice is done, stirring every 8 minutes.

This casserole is very juicy immediately after microwaving. Stir and let stand, uncovered, 5 minutes before serving. Yield: 6 servings (163 calories per serving).

Total Microwave Cooking Time 16 to 23 Minutes

PROTEIN 4.8 / FAT 2.9 / CARBOHYDRATE 29.8 / SODIUM 1164 / CHOLESTEROL 4

After microwaving, remove cover and let stand a few minutes before serving.

Cheesy Vegetable Rice

1 ½ cups long grain
   white rice, cooked
2 cups mozzarella cheese,
   shredded, divided
2 small zucchini, thinly
   sliced
1 medium tomato, chopped
1 green onion, chopped
¼ cup celery, chopped
1 teaspoon Italian herb
   seasoning
1 (8 oz.) carton sour cream

In 1 ½-quart casserole, place rice. In layers over rice, place 1 cup cheese, zucchini, tomato, green onion, celery, Italian seasoning and remaining cheese. Cover. Microwave at MEDIUM HIGH (7) 9 ½ to 15 minutes. Spread sour cream evenly over top. Cover. Microwave at MEDIUM HIGH (7) 1 ½ minutes. Let stand 5 minutes before serving. Yield: 4 servings (495 calories per serving).

Total Microwave Cooking Time 11 to 17 Minutes

PROTEIN 17.9 / FAT 24.8 / CARBOHYDRATE 50.1 / SODIUM 840 / CHOLESTEROL 69

Fettuccine with Onions and Bacon

1 tablespoon butter
½ cup onion, chopped
1 clove garlic, minced
3 slices bacon, chopped
½ cup whipping cream
2 tablespoons grated
   Parmesan cheese
2 tablespoons fresh parsley,
   snipped
½ teaspoon black pepper
¼ teaspoon salt
1 (8 oz.) pkg. fettuccine,
   cooked and drained
1 tablespoon grated
   Parmesan cheese

In 1½-quart casserole, place butter, onion, garlic and bacon. Microwave at HIGH (10) 3 to 4 minutes; stir after 2 minutes. Drain. Add cream, Parmesan cheese, parsley, pepper, salt and fettuccine. Mix well. Microwave at HIGH (10) 1½ to 3 minutes until heated through. Sprinkle with remaining Parmesan cheese. Yield: 4 servings (347 calories per serving).

Total Microwave Cooking Time 4 to 7 Minutes

PROTEIN 11.2 / FAT 13.3 / CARBOHYDRATE 45.5 / SODIUM 346 / CHOLESTEROL 36

Pastas, Cereals & Grains

▲ *Pasta Salad*

Pasta Salad

2 cups fresh snow peas
⅓ cup water
2 cups broccoli flowerets
⅓ cup water
2½ cups cherry tomatoes, halved
2 cups fresh mushrooms, sliced
½ cup ripe olives, halved
3 oz. pasta twists, cooked
1 cup hot pepper cheese, cubed
1 tablespoon grated Parmesan cheese

Pasta Salad Dressing:

½ cup green onions, chopped
½ cup red wine vinegar
½ cup olive oil
1½ teaspoons Dijon mustard
2 tablespoons fresh parsley, snipped
2 cloves garlic, minced
1 teaspoon basil
1 teaspoon dillweed
1 teaspoon salt
1 teaspoon sugar
½ teaspoon white pepper
½ teaspoon oregano

In 2-quart casserole, place snow peas and ⅛ cup water. Cover. Microwave at HIGH (10) 2 minutes. Rinse in cold water immediately. Drain and set aside. Repeat same procedure with broccoli. Drain. In a large bowl, combine snow peas, broccoli, tomatoes, mushrooms, olives, pasta, hot pepper cheese and Parmesan cheese. Set aside.

In a jar, combine green onion, vinegar, olive oil, mustard, parsley, garlic, basil, dillweed, salt, sugar, pepper and oregano. Cover tightly. Shake vigorously until well mixed. Pour over salad mixture and toss well. Chill several hours before serving. Yield: 12 servings (194 calories per serving).

Total Microwave Cooking Time 4 Minutes

PROTEIN 5.2 / FAT 14.9 / CARBOHYDRATE 11.3 / SODIUM 331 / CHOLESTEROL 8

Spaghetti-Cheese Casserole

1 (10 ¾ oz.) can cream of
  mushroom soup
½ cup milk
½ cup sliced stuffed olives
1 teaspoon instant
  minced onion
⅛ teaspoon pepper
1 (7 oz.) pkg. spaghetti,
  cooked and drained
2 cups Cheddar cheese,
  cubed

In small bowl, combine soup, milk, olives, onion and pepper.

In greased 1½-quart casserole alternate layers of spaghetti, cheese and soup mixture. Microwave at HIGH (10) 7 to 12 minutes. Yield: 4 servings (511 calories per serving).

Total Microwave Cooking Time 7 to 12 Minutes

PROTEIN 22.2 / FAT 27.3 / CARBOHYDRATE 43.6 / SODIUM 1122 / CHOLESTEROL 65

Creamy Macaroni and Cheese

¼ cup butter
6 tablespoons all-purpose
  flour
1 teaspoon salt
2 cups milk
2 cups sharp Cheddar
  cheese, shredded
1 (7 oz.) pkg. elbow
  macaroni, cooked and
  drained

In 4-cup glass measure, place butter. Microwave at HIGH (10) ½ to 1 minute until melted.

Blend in flour and salt. Stir in milk until smooth. Microwave at HIGH (10) 4 to 6 minutes, stirring every minute until thickened. Add cheese; stir until completely melted.

In 2-quart casserole, combine cheese sauce and macaroni, mixing well. Microwave at MEDIUM HIGH (7) 5 to 10 minutes, stirring every 3 minutes. Yield: 6 servings (462 calories per serving).

Total Microwave Cooking Time 9½ to 17 Minutes

PROTEIN 18.4 / FAT 23.7 / CARBOHYDRATE 43.3 / SODIUM 743 / CHOLESTEROL 72

Quick and Easy Macaroni and Cheese

1 (16 oz.) pkg. pasteurized
  processed cheese
  spread, cubed
1 (7 oz.) pkg. elbow
  macaroni, cooked and
  drained
1 (5 oz.) can evaporated
  milk

In 2-quart casserole, combine cheese, macaroni and milk. Microwave at HIGH (10) 5 to 8 minutes until cheese is melted and mixture is bubbly, stirring after 3 minutes. Stir before serving. Yield: 6 servings (482 calories per serving).

Total Microwave Cooking Time 5 to 8 Minutes

PROTEIN 24.0 / FAT 26.3 / CARBOHYDRATE 36.8 / SODIUM 1109 / CHOLESTEROL 78

Pastas, Cereals & Grains

▲ *Ripe Olive Risotto*

Ripe Olive Risotto

2 cups chicken broth
1 cup long grain rice
1 cup onion,
   finely chopped
⅓ cup celery, chopped
¼ cup butter
1 teaspoon salt
¼ teaspoon pepper
½ cup ripe olives, chopped
1 (4 oz.) can sliced
   mushrooms, drained
1 (2 oz.) jar sliced pimento,
   drained
¼ cup grated
   Parmesan cheese

In 2-quart casserole combine broth, rice, onion, celery, butter, salt and pepper. Cover. Microwave at HIGH (10) 15 to 20 minutes until liquid is absorbed, stirring after 10 minutes.

Add olives, mushrooms, pimento and cheese; mix well. Microwave at HIGH (10) 1 to 3 minutes. Stir before serving. Yield: 8 servings (165 calories per serving).

Total Microwave Cooking Time 16 to 23 Minutes

PROTEIN 5.8 / FAT 8.2 / CARBOHYDRATE 16.9 / SODIUM 1122 / CHOLESTEROL 18

Pilaf

1 cup instant rice
1 cup water
⅓ cup onion, chopped
⅓ cup green pepper,
   chopped
⅓ cup carrots, shredded
⅓ cup celery, chopped
3 tablespoons butter
1 tablespoon instant beef
   bouillon granules
¼ teaspoon cumin
⅛ teaspoon coriander
Dash pepper

In 1 ½ -quart casserole, combine rice, water, onion, green pepper, carrots, celery, butter, beef bouillon, cumin, coriander and pepper. Cover. Microwave at HIGH (10) 6 to 10 minutes; stir after 4 minutes. Let stand, covered, 5 minutes before serving. Yield: 4 servings (229 calories per serving).

Total Microwave Cooking Time 6 to 10 Minutes

PROTEIN 3.8 / FAT 9.2 / CARBOHYDRATE 32.5 / SODIUM 556 / CHOLESTEROL 23

Jiffy Spanish Rice

1 lb. lean ground beef
1 cup instant rice
1 (28 oz.) can tomatoes,
   cut up
1 tablespoon instant
   minced onion
1 tablespoon chili powder
1 teaspoon salt
⅛ teaspoon pepper

In 2-quart casserole, crumble beef. Microwave at HIGH (10) 4 to 6 minutes, stirring after 3 minutes. Drain. Add rice, tomatoes, onion, chili powder, salt and pepper. Cover. Microwave at HIGH (10) 7 to 11 minutes, stirring after 4 minutes. Stir well. Let stand, covered, 5 minutes before serving. Yield: 4 servings (405 calories per serving).

Total Microwave Cooking Time 11 to 17 Minutes

PROTEIN 20.0 / FAT 18.6 / CARBOHYDRATE 38.8 / SODIUM 1378 / CHOLESTEROL 64

Noodles Romanoff

1 (8 oz.) pkg. narrow
   noodles, cooked and
   drained
1 cup cottage cheese
1 (8 oz.) carton sour cream
¼ cup stuffed olives,
   chopped
1 teaspoon instant
   minced onion
½ teaspoon salt
½ teaspoon
   Worcestershire sauce
Dash hot sauce
1 cup sharp Cheddar
   cheese, shredded

In 2-quart casserole, combine noodles, cottage cheese, sour cream, olives, onion, salt, Worcestershire sauce and hot sauce. Mix well. Cover. Microwave at HIGH (10) 6 to 8 minutes until hot, stirring after 4 minutes. Sprinkle cheese on top. Microwave at HIGH (10) 1 to 3 minutes, uncovered, until cheese melts. Yield: 6 servings (333 calories per serving).

Total Microwave Cooking Time 7 to 11 Minutes

PROTEIN 15.1 / FAT 16.9 / CARBOHYDRATE 29.8 / SODIUM 540 / CHOLESTEROL 42

Granola

2½ cups regular rolled
   oats
½ cup coconut
½ cup peanuts, coarsely
   chopped
⅓ cup sunflower seeds
⅓ cup toasted wheat germ
¾ cup honey or molasses
¼ cup oil
¾ cup mixed dried fruit
   bits
½ cup pitted dates,
   chopped
½ cup miniature chocolate
   chips

In large mixing bowl, combine rolled oats, coconut, peanuts, sunflower seeds and wheat germ. Set aside. In small mixing bowl, combine honey and oil. Pour over oat mixture, stirring well to coat evenly. Microwave at HIGH (10) 5 to 10 minutes until mixture is toasted, stirring every 2 minutes. Add dried fruit bits, dates and chocolate chips. Set aside. Line 3-quart oblong glass baking dish with foil. Press the granola mixture into dish. Cool and break into pieces. Store in an airtight container. Yield: 7 cups (577 calories per cup).

Total Microwave Cooking Time 5 to 10 Minutes

PROTEIN 12.0 / FAT 24.6 / CARBOHYDRATE 86.3 / SODIUM 68 / CHOLESTEROL 0

After cooling, break into pieces and store in airtight container.

Quick Breads

Cranberry-Orange Muffins

2 cups all-purpose flour
½ cup sugar
1 tablespoon baking
  powder
¼ teaspoon salt
2 eggs, beaten
½ cup oil
½ cup milk
½ cup fresh cranberries,
  coarsely chopped
1 teaspoon grated
  orange rind
1 tablespoon sugar
1 teaspoon cinnamon

In large mixing bowl, combine flour, ½ cup sugar, baking powder and salt. Make a well in center of dry mixture. Combine eggs, oil and milk. Add egg mixture, cranberries and orange rind to dry ingredients. Stir just until moistened. Spoon into paper-lined microwave-safe muffin pan, filling each cup about half full. Combine 1 tablespoon sugar and cinnamon. Sprinkle evenly over batter. Microwave at MEDIUM HIGH (7) 2 to 4 minutes. Repeat with remaining batter. Yield: 18 muffins (144 calories each).

Total Microwave Cooking Time 2 to 4 Minutes

PROTEIN 2.5 / FAT 7.1 / CARBOHYDRATE 17.8 / SODIUM 95 / CHOLESTEROL 30

Raisin Bran Muffins

2 cups whole bran cereal
1½ cups all-purpose flour
1 cup sugar
1 cup raisins
1 tablespoon plus
  2 teaspoons
  baking powder
½ teaspoon salt
2 eggs, beaten
1½ cups milk
½ cup oil

In large mixing bowl, stir together cereal, flour, sugar, raisins, baking powder and salt. Make a well in center of dry mixture. Combine eggs, milk and oil. Add egg mixture to dry ingredients. Stir just until moistened. Spoon into paper-lined, microwave-safe muffin pan, filling each cup about half full. Microwave at MEDIUM HIGH (7) 2 to 4 minutes. Repeat with remaining batter. Yield: 24 muffins (151 calories each).

Total Microwave Cooking Time 2 to 4 Minutes

PROTEIN 2.8 / FAT 5.9 / CARBOHYDRATE 24.0 / SODIUM 164 / CHOLESTEROL 24

Pumpkin Bread

¼ cup graham cracker
  crumbs
1⅓ cups all-purpose flour
1⅓ cups sugar
1 cup canned pumpkin
⅓ cup water
⅓ cup shortening
2 eggs
1 teaspoon baking soda
1 teaspoon pumpkin
  pie spice
¾ teaspoon salt
⅓ cup pecans,
  coarsely chopped
⅓ cup golden raisins
2 teaspoons grated
  orange rind

Generously grease a 9-cup microwave-safe ring mold; coat with graham cracker crumbs. In medium mixing bowl, combine flour, sugar, pumpkin, water, shortening, eggs, baking soda, pumpkin pie spice and salt; beat until smooth. Stir in nuts, raisins and orange rind. Pour into ring mold. Microwave at HIGH (10) 8 to 14 minutes. Let stand 10 minutes before removing from pan. Yield: 8 servings (372 calories per serving).

Total Microwave Cooking Time 8 to 14 Minutes

PROTEIN 5.2 / FAT 13.7 / CARBOHYDRATE 59.5 / SODIUM 363 / CHOLESTEROL 65

◀ *Cranberry-Orange Muffins and Bran Raisin Muffins*

Quick Breads

Cranberry Coffee Ring

1 tablespoon butter, melted
1 cup whole berry
    cranberry sauce
¼ cup sugar
¼ cup walnuts, chopped
1½ cups buttermilk
    baking mix
¾ cup orange juice
1 egg, beaten
2 tablespoons sugar
½ teaspoon cinnamon
½ cup powdered sugar
½ teaspoon vanilla
2 to 3 teaspoons water

Line bottom of 9-inch round glass deep pie dish with wax paper. Place a small drinking glass, right side up, in center of dish. Set aside.

In small mixing bowl, combine butter, cranberry sauce, ¼ cup sugar and walnuts. Spread mixture evenly around glass in baking dish.

In medium mixing bowl, combine baking mix, orange juice, egg, 2 tablespoons sugar and cinnamon. Mix well. Spread over cranberry mixture. Microwave at MEDIUM HIGH (7) 6 minutes. Continue microwaving at HIGH (10) 3 to 5 minutes until cake springs back when lightly touched. Let stand 5 minutes. Invert onto serving plate. Cool slightly.

In small bowl, combine powdered sugar and vanilla. Stir in enough water to make desired consistency. Drizzle over cake. Yield: 8 servings (331 calories per serving).

Total Microwave Cooking Time 9 to 12 Minutes

PROTEIN 3.3 / FAT 8.4 / CARBOHYDRATE 55.4 / SODIUM 397 / CHOLESTEROL 13

Traditional Steamed Brown Bread

¾ cup cornmeal
¾ cup whole wheat flour
¾ cup rye flour
1½ teaspoons baking soda
½ teaspoon salt
1¼ cups buttermilk
½ cup dark molasses
¾ cup raisins

In a large mixing bowl, combine cornmeal, whole wheat flour, rye flour, baking soda and salt. Add buttermilk, molasses and raisins. Stir thoroughly.

Grease a 2-quart casserole. Place a small drinking glass, right side up, in center. Pour mixture evenly around glass. Cover dish tightly with plastic wrap. Microwave at MEDIUM (5) 16 to 21 minutes. Unmold and let stand 10 minutes before slicing. Yield: 10 servings (172 calories per serving).

Total Microwave Cooking Time 16 to 21 Minutes

PROTEIN 3.9 / FAT 0.9 / CARBOHYDRATE 38.9 / SODIUM 293 / CHOLESTEROL 1

Orange-Nut Muffins

Fill cups half full so that batter does not overflow during microwaving.

2 cups all-purpose flour
⅓ cup sugar
1 teaspoon baking powder
½ teaspoon baking soda
¼ teaspoon salt
1 cup natural nutty cereal
¾ cup raisins
1 cup orange juice
⅓ cup oil
1½ teaspoons grated
    orange rind

In large mixing bowl, combine flour, sugar, baking powder, baking soda, salt, cereal and raisins. In small bowl, combine orange juice, oil and orange rind; add to dry ingredients. Stir until moistened. Fill paper-lined, microwave-safe muffin cups about half full. Microwave at HIGH (10) 2 to 4 minutes. Repeat with remaining batter. Yield: 15 muffins (177 calories each).

Total Microwave Cooking Time 2 to 4 Minutes

PROTEIN 2.9 / FAT 5.1 / CARBOHYDRATE 31.0 / SODIUM 140 / CHOLESTEROL 0

Apple Spice Bread

1 cup all-purpose flour
¾ cup sugar
¾ teaspoon cinnamon
½ teaspoon baking soda
¼ teaspoon salt
½ cup applesauce
¼ cup butter, melted
1 egg, beaten
2 tablespoons burgundy
  wine

Sift flour, sugar, cinnamon, baking soda and salt together. In medium mixing bowl, combine applesauce, butter, egg and burgundy wine. Add flour mixture and stir until blended. Grease a 9-inch round glass deep pie dish. Fill with batter. Microwave at HIGH (10) 5 to 7 minutes. Cool 15 to 20 minutes. Yield: 8 servings (207 calories per serving).

Total Microwave Cooking Time 5 to 7 Minutes

PROTEIN 2.7 / FAT 6.7 / CARBOHYDRATE 34.0 / SODIUM 194 / CHOLESTEROL 48

Breakfast Banana Bread

½ cup ripe banana,
  mashed
½ cup brown sugar,
  firmly packed
¼ cup oil
¼ cup milk
½ teaspoon vanilla
1 egg, beaten
1 cup self-rising flour
½ cup walnuts, chopped

Topping:
¼ cup brown sugar,
  firmly packed
2 tablespoons all-purpose
  flour
½ teaspoon cinnamon
1 tablespoon butter

In medium mixing bowl, combine banana, ½ cup brown sugar, oil, milk, vanilla and egg. Add 1 cup flour, and walnuts; stir until moistened. Pour into greased 9-inch round glass deep pie dish. Microwave at MEDIUM (5) 5 minutes.

In small mixing bowl, combine ¼ cup brown sugar, 2 tablespoons flour and cinnamon. Cut butter into dry ingredients until mixture is crumbly. Sprinkle on cake. Microwave at HIGH (10) 3 to 5 minutes until center springs back when lightly touched. Let stand 5 to 10 minutes. Yield: 6 servings (387 calories per serving).

Total Microwave Cooking Time 8 to 11 Minutes

PROTEIN 5.6 / FAT 18.9 / CARBOHYDRATE 51.0 / SODIUM 311 / CHOLESTEROL 50

Quick Cherry Caramel Ring

¼ cup butter
½ cup brown sugar,
  firmly packed
2 tablespoons light
  corn syrup
½ cup pecan halves
¼ cup maraschino
  cherries, quartered
1 (10 oz.) pkg. refrigerated
  buttermilk biscuits

Place butter in 9-inch round glass deep pie dish. Microwave at HIGH (10) ½ to 1 minute until melted. Sprinkle brown sugar over butter; add corn syrup and stir well. Place small drinking glass, right side up, in center of dish. Arrange pecans and cherries on bottom of dish around glass.

Place biscuits over nuts and cherries, squeezing to fit. Microwave at MEDIUM (5) 5 to 8 minutes. Remove glass and invert caramel ring onto serving plate. Let stand 2 minutes. Yield: 5 servings (321 calories per serving).

Total Microwave Cooking Time 5 to 8 Minutes

PROTEIN 2.0 / FAT 18.7 / CARBOHYDRATE 37.9 / SODIUM 116 / CHOLESTEROL 25

Place small drinking glass in center of dish to make a baking ring.

Quick Breads

▲ *Savory Corn Bread*

Savory Corn Bread

½ (3 oz.) can French-fried
   onions, finely crushed
1 tablespoon grated
   Parmesan cheese
1 cup yellow cornmeal
1 cup all-purpose flour
2 tablespoons sugar
4 teaspoons baking powder
¼ teaspoon salt
1 egg
1 cup milk
½ cup oil

Combine onions and Parmesan cheese. Place mixture in well-greased 9-inch microwave-safe baking ring. Turn ring to coat sides and bottom; set aside.

In large mixing bowl, combine cornmeal, flour, sugar, baking powder and salt. Add egg, milk and oil; stir until smooth. Pour batter into prepared baking ring. Microwave at MEDIUM (5) 6 to 10 minutes until done. Invert onto serving plate. Fill center of ring with cooked fresh vegetables before serving, if desired. Yield: 6 servings (401 calories per serving).

Total Microwave Cooking Time 6 to 10 Minutes

PROTEIN 5.9 / FAT 24.4 / CARBOHYDRATE 40.7 / SODIUM 375 / CHOLESTEROL 7

Basic Nut Bread

2 ½ cups all-purpose flour
1 cup sugar
1 tablespoon
   baking powder
½ teaspoon salt
1 ¼ cups milk
1 egg
3 tablespoons oil
1 ¼ cups nuts,
   finely chopped, divided

In large mixing bowl, combine flour, sugar, baking powder and salt. Combine milk, egg and oil; beat well. Add milk mixture and 1 cup nuts to flour mixture; stir just until moistened.

Generously grease a 10-inch microwave-safe fluted ring mold. Sprinkle remaining nuts over bottom. Pour batter into prepared ring mold. Microwave at MEDIUM HIGH (7) 9 to 13 minutes, rotating ¼ turn after 6 minutes. Let stand 5 minutes; invert onto cooling rack. Serve warm. Yield: 8 servings (488 calories per serving).

Total Microwave Cooking Time 9 to 13 Minutes

PROTEIN 8.9 / FAT 19.1 / CARBOHYDRATE 72.7 / SODIUM 290 / CHOLESTEROL 38

Everyday Coffee Cake

1 ½ cups buttermilk
   baking mix
¼ cup sugar
½ cup milk
1 egg
2 tablespoons oil
⅓ cup buttermilk
   baking mix
⅓ cup brown sugar,
   firmly packed
2 tablespoons butter
1 teaspoon cinnamon
¼ cup nuts, chopped

In mixing bowl, combine 1½ cups baking mix and sugar. Add milk, egg and oil; mix well. Pour batter into greased 8-inch square glass baking dish.

Combine ⅓ cup baking mix, brown sugar, butter and cinnamon; stir with fork until crumbly. Stir in nuts. Sprinkle evenly over batter. Microwave at MEDIUM HIGH (7) 6 to 9 minutes until wooden pick inserted in center comes out clean. Cool 15 minutes and drizzle with Vanilla Glaze. Yield: 8 servings (335 calories per serving).

Vanilla Glaze: Combine ¾ cup powdered sugar, 1 tablespoon milk and 1 teaspoon vanilla; stir well. Drizzle over coffee cake.

Total Microwave Cooking Time 6 to 9 Minutes

PROTEIN 5.0 / FAT 15.4 / CARBOHYDRATE 45.1 / SODIUM 503 / CHOLESTEROL 48

Coffee cake is done when a wooden pick inserted in center comes out clean.

Mushroom Stuffing

½ lb. fresh mushrooms,
   sliced
½ cup onion, chopped
½ cup celery, chopped
½ cup butter
1 egg, beaten
1 (8 oz.) pkg. seasoned
   stuffing mix
1 cup hot water
2 teaspoons instant
   chicken bouillon
   granules
1 teaspoon sage
½ teaspoon pepper

In 2-quart casserole, combine mushrooms, onion, celery and butter. Microwave at HIGH (10) 4 to 7 minutes until vegetables are tender. Add egg, stuffing mix, water, bouillon, sage and pepper. Microwave at HIGH (10) 4 to 6 minutes until heated through; stir after 2 minutes. Yield: 8 servings (234 calories per serving).

Total Microwave Cooking Time 8 to 13 Minutes

PROTEIN 5.7 / FAT 13.9 / CARBOHYDRATE 23.2 / SODIUM 981 / CHOLESTEROL 64

Desserts & Candies

Fruit Tart

Pastry Cream:
2 cups milk
½ cup sugar
¼ cup all-purpose flour
2 egg yolks, beaten
1 tablespoon butter
2 teaspoons vanilla

Fruit topping:
4 kiwi fruits, peeled and
   sliced
1 pint raspberries
1 pint strawberries, halved
   lengthwise
1 (11 oz.) can Mandarin
   oranges, drained
1 (9-inch) baked
   tart shell
½ cup apricot preserves,
   warmed

Place milk in medium mixing bowl and Microwave at MEDIUM HIGH (7) 6 to 8 minutes until milk is steaming. Add sugar and flour. Microwave at HIGH (10) 2 to 3 minutes, stirring every 30 seconds. Add egg yolks, butter and vanilla. Microwave at HIGH (10) 2 to 3 minutes, stirring every 30 seconds. Cover with plastic wrap and refrigerate until chilled.

Spread pastry cream in tart shell. Arrange fruit over cream. Brush fruit lightly with apricot preserves. Yield: 8 servings (379 calories each).

Total Microwave Cooking Time 10 to 14 Minutes

PROTEIN 6.3 / FAT 12.7 / CARBOHYDRATE 61.7 / SODIUM 176 / CHOLESTEROL 67

Baked Fruit

1 orange
1 lemon
1 (16 oz.) can sliced
   peaches, drained
1 (16 oz.) can pear
   halves, drained
1 (16 oz.) can apricots,
   drained
1 (15 ¼ oz.) can pineapple
   slices, drained
⅓ cup raisins
1 (6 oz.) jar maraschino
   cherries, drained
1 cup brown sugar,
   firmly packed
1 teaspoon cinnamon
2 tablespoons all-purpose
   flour
1 tablespoon angostura
   bitters

Grate rind of orange and lemon. Remove remaining peel and thinly slice fruit. In 2-quart casserole, layer orange slices, lemon slices, peaches, pears, apricots, pineapple, raisins and maraschino cherries.

In small mixing bowl, combine orange and lemon rind, brown sugar, cinnamon, flour and angostura bitters; mix well and sprinkle over fruit. Microwave at HIGH (10) 11 to 13 minutes until bubbly. Serve warm. Yield: 12 servings (142 calories each).

Total Microwave Cooking Time 11 to 13 Minutes

PROTEIN 1.1 / FAT 0.1 / CARBOHYDRATE 36.9 / SODIUM 13 / CHOLESTEROL 0

Desserts & Candies

▲ *White Chocolate Cheesecake*

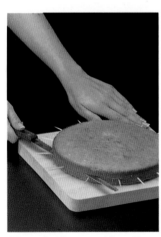

Use toothpicks as a guide to slice cake evenly.

Boston Cream Pie

1 (9 oz.) pkg. yellow cake mix

Filling:
½ cup sugar
2 tablespoons cornstarch
1⅔ cups milk
1 egg, beaten
¾ teaspoon vanilla
¼ teaspoon butter flavoring
1 cup whipping cream, whipped

Glaze:
2 (1 oz.) squares unsweetened chocolate
2 tablespoons butter
1¼ cups powdered sugar, sifted
1¼ teaspoons vanilla
3 to 4 tablespoons hot water

Prepare layer cake according to package directions. Cool completely and cut into 2 thin layers.

In 2-quart casserole, combine sugar, cornstarch and milk. Stir well with a wire whisk. Microwave at HIGH (10) 3 to 6 minutes, until thickened, stirring every 2 minutes. Stir small amount of hot mixture into beaten egg. Add egg mixture, vanilla and butter flavoring to hot mixture. Microwave at MEDIUM HIGH (7) 1 minute. Cool completely. Fold whipped cream into thickened mixture. Spread filling between cake layers.

In 4-cup glass measure, combine chocolate and butter. Microwave at HIGH (10) 1 to 2 minutes until chocolate is melted. Add powdered sugar and vanilla. Blend in hot water; 1 tablespoon at a time, until glaze is desired consistency. Spread over top and sides of cake. Yield: 8 servings (479 calories each).

Total Microwave Cooking Time 5 to 9 Minutes

PROTEIN 5.6 / FAT 25.5 / CARBOHYDRATE 60.6 / SODIUM 195 / CHOLESTEROL 88

White Chocolate Cheesecake

1½ cups graham cracker
   crumbs
¼ cup ground almonds,
   toasted
¼ cup plus 1 tablespoon
   butter, melted
1 pound white chocolate,
   coarsely chopped
2 (8 oz.) pkgs.
   cream cheese, softened
½ cup sour cream
3 eggs
1 teaspoon vanilla
½ teaspoon almond
   extract
Melted chocolate, optional
Strawberries, optional

Combine graham cracker crumbs, almonds and butter; blend well. Press mixture onto bottom and 1 inch up sides of 9-inch springform pan. Chill.

Place white chocolate in 1-quart casserole. Microwave at MEDIUM (5) 2 to 3 minutes. Stir until smooth. Cool slightly. Combine cream cheese and sour cream in a large mixing bowl; beat at medium speed of an electric mixer until fluffy. Add eggs, one at a time, beating well after each addition. Add vanilla, almond extract and chocolate; stir until smooth and well blended. Pour mixture into 2-quart casserole. Microwave at MEDIUM HIGH (7) 8 to 11 minutes until very thick, stirring with wire whisk every 2 minutes. Pour into crust. Refrigerate 4 hours. Drizzle chocolate over top and garnish with chocolate-dipped strawberries, if desired. Yield: 12 servings (467 calories each).

Total Microwave Cooking Time 10 to 14 Minutes

PROTEIN 7.9 / FAT 36.6 / CARBOHYDRATE 33.1 / SODIUM 257 / CHOLESTEROL 124

Dip lower half of strawberry into melted chocolate. Place on foil-lined tray; refrigerate.

Bread Pudding with Bourbon Sauce

4 cups bread cubes
   (4 to 5 slices)
½ cup brown sugar,
   firmly packed
½ cup raisins
½ teaspoon nutmeg
¼ teaspoon salt
2 cups milk
¼ cup butter
2 eggs, beaten

Bourbon Sauce:
½ cup sugar
1 tablespoon cornstarch
½ teaspoon cinnamon
½ cup hot water
¼ cup bourbon
2 tablespoons butter

Spread bread cubes evenly in 8-inch round microwave-safe dish. Combine brown sugar, raisins, nutmeg and salt. Sprinkle evenly over bread cubes. Set aside.

Place milk and butter in 4-cup glass measure. Microwave at HIGH (10) 4 minutes until butter is melted and milk is warm. Rapidly stir in eggs with a fork and blend well. Pour milk mixture over bread cubes. Microwave at MEDIUM HIGH (7) 9 to 12 minutes until center is set. Yield: 6 servings (435 calories each).

Bourbon Sauce: Combine sugar, cornstarch and cinnamon in 1-quart casserole. Combine water and bourbon. Gradually add to sugar mixture, stirring until smooth. Microwave at HIGH (10) 3 to 4 minutes, stirring once. Add butter and stir until blended. Serve warm over Bread Pudding.

Total Microwave Cooking Time 16 to 20 Minutes

PROTEIN 7.5 / FAT 17.0 / CARBOHYDRATE 59.8 / SODIUM 393 / CHOLESTEROL 129

Desserts & Candies

▲ *Three Layer Brownies and Sweet-Tart Lemon Squares*

Three Layer Brownies

¾ **cup quick-cooking oats**
⅓ **cup all-purpose flour**
⅓ **cup brown sugar,**
   firmly packed
¼ **teaspoon baking soda**
¼ **cup butter, melted**
1 **(1 oz.) square**
   unsweetened chocolate
4 **tablespoons butter**
⅓ **cup granulated sugar**
2 **tablespoons water**
1 **egg, beaten**
¾ **teaspoon vanilla**
½ **cup all-purpose flour**
¼ **teaspoon baking powder**
½ **cup pecans, chopped**

Frosting:
1 **(1 oz.) square**
   unsweetened chocolate
1 **tablespoon butter**
1 **cup powdered sugar,**
   sifted
½ **teaspoon almond extract**
2 **tablespoons hot water**

In small mixing bowl, combine oats, ⅛ cup flour, brown sugar, baking soda and ¼ cup butter. Press mixture into 8-inch square glass baking dish. Microwave at MEDIUM (5) 2 to 4 minutes until surface appears dry. Let cool on wire rack 10 minutes. In 2-quart casserole, combine chocolate and 4 tablespoons butter. Microwave at HIGH (10) 2 to 3 minutes until melted. Add granulated sugar, water, egg, vanilla, flour, baking powder and pecans. Mix well. Spread mixture evenly over oat mixture. Microwave at MEDIUM (5) 5 to 7 minutes. Let cool. Frost with Chocolate Frosting.

Chocolate Frosting: In 1-quart casserole, combine chocolate and butter. Microwave at HIGH (10) 1 to 2 minutes until melted. Add powdered sugar and almond extract. Add hot water, 1 tablespoon at a time, until frosting is spreadable. Yield: 2 dozen bars (137 calories each).

Total Microwave Cooking Time 10 to 16 Minutes

PROTEIN 1.7 / FAT 7.6 / CARBOHYDRATE 16.9 / SODIUM 60 / CHOLESTEROL 22

Basic Brownies

1 cup sugar
2 eggs
½ teaspoon salt
1 teaspoon vanilla
½ cup butter, melted
¾ cup all-purpose flour
½ cup cocoa
1 cup nuts, chopped

In small bowl at medium speed of electric mixer, beat together sugar, eggs, salt and vanilla 1 minute or until light. Add melted butter. Continue beating until thoroughly blended. Mix in flour and cocoa at low speed. Stir in nuts. Spread evenly in greased 8-inch square glass baking dish. Microwave at HIGH (10) 5 to 7 minutes. When done, top looks dry and will spring back when lightly touched. Cut when cool. Yield: 16 squares (188 calories each).

Total Microwave Cooking Time 5 to 7 Minutes

PROTEIN 3.1 / FAT 11.7 / CARBOHYDRATE 19.9 / SODIUM 143 / CHOLESTEROL 48

Turtle Cake

25 caramel candies, unwrapped
¼ cup evaporated milk
1 (9 oz.) pkg. chocolate cake mix
¼ cup butter, melted
2 tablespoons evaporated milk
½ cup semisweet chocolate chips
½ cup pecans, chopped

In medium mixing bowl, combine caramels and ¼ cup evaporated milk. Microwave at HIGH (10) 2 to 3 minutes, stirring every 30 seconds. In large mixing bowl, combine cake mix, butter, and 2 tablespoons evaporated milk. Press one-half of cake mixture into lightly greased 8-inch square glass baking dish. Microwave at HIGH (10) 1 to 2 minutes. Sprinkle chocolate chips and pecans on top. Spread caramel mixture over chocolate chips and pecans. Crumble remaining cake mix over caramel mixture. Microwave at HIGH (10) 3 to 4 minutes. Cool before cutting. Yield: 10 servings (252 calories each).

Total Microwave Cooking Time 6 to 9 Minutes

PROTEIN 2.7 / FAT 13.4 / CARBOHYDRATE 34.2 / SODIUM 174 / CHOLESTEROL 13

Sweet-Tart Lemon Squares

1 (14 oz.) can sweetened condensed milk
½ cup lemon juice
1 teaspoon grated lemon rind
1½ cups graham cracker crumbs
⅓ cup brown sugar, firmly packed
¼ cup butter, melted

In small mixing bowl, stir together milk, lemon juice and lemon rind until thick and smooth. Set aside.

Combine graham cracker crumbs, sugar and butter; blend well. Firmly press ⅔ of crumb mixture into bottom of 8-inch square glass baking dish. Spread lemon mixture evenly over crumbs. Sprinkle with remaining crumbs. Microwave at HIGH (10) 5 to 7 minutes. Cool and cut into squares. Yield: 16 squares (154 calories each).

Total Microwave Cooking Time 5 to 7 Minutes

PROTEIN 2.7 / FAT 5.8 / CARBOHYDRATE 24.3 / SODIUM 117 / CHOLESTEROL 16

Desserts & Candies

▲ *Fruit-Filled Pineapple*

Fruit-Filled Pineapple

Cut out fruit in chunks, leaving ¼-inch shell. Remove and discard core.

1 medium-size fresh pineapple
1 (11 oz.) can Mandarin oranges, drained
1 cup shredded coconut
½ cup maraschino cherries, drained and cut in half
½ cup orange marmalade
½ cup almonds, sliced, toasted
2 tablespoons light rum

Cut leafy crown off pineapple; reserve for garnish, if desired. Cut pineapple in half lengthwise. Scoop out fruit, leaving 1/4-inch shell. Remove woody core from fruit and discard. Cut remaining fruit into chunks.

Combine pineapple chunks, oranges, coconut, cherries, marmalade, almonds, and rum; toss gently. Place shells in 2-quart oblong glass baking dish. Divide fruit mixture evenly between shells. Cover with wax paper. Microwave at High (10) 7 to 9 minutes or until heated through. Yield: 6 servings (298 calories per serving).

Total Microwave Cooking Time 7 to 9 Minutes

PROTEIN 3.7 / FAT 12.0 / CARBOHYDRATE 46.6 / SODIUM 49 / CHOLESTEROL 0

Bananas Foster

3 medium bananas, peeled
Lemon juice
½ cup pecan halves
½ cup brown sugar,
  firmly packed
3 tablespoons butter
2 tablespoons orange juice
½ teaspoon vanilla
2 tablespoons light rum,
  optional
Vanilla ice cream

Slice bananas in half crosswise and then lengthwise; place in 9-inch pie plate. Brush with lemon juice and sprinkle with pecans. In 2-cup glass measure, combine brown sugar, butter, orange juice and vanilla. Microwave at HIGH (10) 1 minute. Pour sauce over bananas. Microwave at HIGH (10) 1 to 3 minutes until bananas are warm. Add rum, if desired. Serve warm with ice cream. Yield: 4 servings (491 calories per serving).

Total Microwave Cooking Time 2 to 4 Minutes

PROTEIN 4.4 / FAT 25.3 / CARBOHYDRATE 66.8 / SODIUM 156 / CHOLESTEROL 53

Apple Crisp

6 cups apples, peeled,
  sliced
¾ cup brown sugar,
  firmly packed
½ cup all-purpose flour
⅓ cup brown sugar,
  firmly packed
⅓ cup quick-cooking oats
¼ cup butter
½ teaspoon cinnamon

In 8-inch square glass baking dish, place apples and ¾ cup sugar.
Combine flour, ⅓ cup sugar, oats, butter and cinnamon. Mix with pastry blender or fork until crumbly. Sprinkle over apple mixture. Microwave at HIGH (10) 7 to 12 minutes. Let stand 5 minutes before serving. Yield: 8 servings (251 calories per serving).

Total Microwave Cooking Time 7 to 12 Minutes

PROTEIN 1.5 / FAT 6.3 / CARBOHYDRATE 49.3 / SODIUM 68 / CHOLESTEROL 16

Easy Peach Cobbler

1 (20 oz.) can peach
  pie filling
½ teaspoon almond
  extract
1 (9 oz.) pkg. yellow cake
  mix
¼ cup butter, thinly sliced
¼ cup almonds, chopped,
  toasted
2 tablespoons sugar
½ teaspoon cinnamon
⅛ teaspoon ginger

Combine pie filling and almond extract. Spread peach mixture in 8-inch square glass baking dish. Microwave at HIGH (10) 3 to 4 minutes until heated through. Sprinkle cake mix over peach filling. Arrange butter slices evenly over cake mix.
Combine almonds, sugar, cinnamon and ginger; sprinkle over top. Microwave at HIGH (10) 12 to 14 minutes. Yield: 6 servings (452 calories per serving).

Total Microwave Cooking Time 15 to 18 Minutes

PROTEIN 3.7 / FAT 18.2 / CARBOHYDRATE 72.0 / SODIUM 270 / CHOLESTEROL 21

Desserts & Candies

▲ *Carrot Cake*

Carrot Cake

1½ cups sugar
1 cup oil
1 teaspoon vanilla
3 eggs
1½ cups all-purpose flour
1¼ teaspoons baking soda
2½ teaspoons cinnamon
¼ teaspoon salt
2¼ cups raw carrots, grated
½ cup pecans, chopped

Glaze:
1 (3 oz.) pkg. cream cheese, softened
½ cup sifted powdered sugar
¼ teaspoon vanilla
1 to 3 teaspoons milk

In large mixing bowl, blend sugar, oil, vanilla and eggs. Beat at medium speed of electric mixer for one minute.

In small bowl, stir together flour, soda, cinnamon and salt. Add to sugar-egg mixture and mix on low speed for 1 minute. Fold in carrots and pecans. Pour batter into well-greased 10-inch microwave-safe bundt pan. Microwave at HIGH (10) 11 to 16 minutes. Let cake stand 10 minutes before removing from pan. Drizzle with glaze. Yield: 16 servings (318 calories each).

Glaze: In small bowl, combine cream cheese, powdered sugar and vanilla. Add milk, 1 teaspoon at a time, until drizzling consistency is reached. Drizzle on warm cake.

Total Microwave Cooking Time 11 to 16 Minutes

PROTEIN 3.5 / FAT 19.2 / CARBOHYDRATE 34.3 / SODIUM 137 / CHOLESTEROL 54

Pineapple Upside Down Cake

¼ cup butter
⅓ cup brown sugar,
    firmly packed
1 (8 oz.) can pineapple
    slices
4 maraschino cherries,
    cut in half
1¼ cups all-purpose flour
¾ cup sugar
2 teaspoons baking powder
½ teaspoon salt
⅓ cup shortening
1 egg
Pineapple liquid plus
    milk to total ½ cup
1 teaspoon vanilla

In 8-inch round microwave-safe dish, place butter. Microwave at HIGH (10) ¾ to 1 minute to melt. Sprinkle sugar over butter. Drain pineapple, reserving liquid. Arrange pineapple slices in dish. Decorate with cherries.

In small mixer bowl, place flour, sugar, baking powder, salt, shortening, egg, pineapple-milk mixture and vanilla. Beat 3 minutes on lowest mixer speed. Carefully spread batter over fruit in dish.

Microwave at HIGH (10) 8 to 12 minutes. (Some batter may run onto edges of dish, but will not spill.) When done, toothpick inserted in center of cake comes out clean. Invert cake onto plate; let dish stand over cake 5 minutes. Serve hot or warm. Yield: 8 servings (327 calories each).

Total Microwave Cooking Time 8 to 13 Minutes

PROTEIN 2.3 / FAT 14.7 / CARBOHYDRATE 47.5 / SODIUM 286 / CHOLESTEROL 17

Banana Buttermilk Cake

2½ cups all-purpose flour
1 cup brown sugar,
    firmly packed
¾ cup sugar
½ cup walnuts, chopped
1 teaspoon cinnamon
½ teaspoon salt
¾ cup oil
2 eggs
1 cup bananas, mashed
⅔ cup buttermilk
1 teaspoon baking powder
1 teaspoon baking soda
1 cup powdered sugar
¼ cup butter, melted
1 teaspoon vanilla

In large mixing bowl, combine flour, brown sugar, sugar, nuts, cinnamon, salt and oil to make a crumbly mixture. Spread ¾ cup mixture in bottom of a well-greased 10-cup bundt pan.

To remaining mixture, add eggs, bananas, buttermilk, baking powder and baking soda. Stir until smooth. Pour over crumb mixture.

Microwave at HIGH (10) 9 to 12 minutes. Cool 15 minutes before removing from pan.

Combine powdered sugar, butter and vanilla; stir until smooth. Drizzle over warm cake. Yield: 12 servings (395 calories each).

Total Microwave Cooking Time 9 to 12 Minutes

PROTEIN 2.7 / FAT 21.5 / CARBOHYDRATE 50.3 / SODIUM 268 / CHOLESTEROL 47

Desserts & Candies

Marshmallow Crisp

¼ cup butter
1 (10 oz.) pkg. large marshmallows (about 40)
5 cups crispy rice cereal

In 3-quart casserole place butter. Microwave at HIGH (10) 1 minute to melt. Add marshmallows. Cover. Microwave at HIGH (10) 2 to 3 minutes. Stir until butter is melted and marshmallows are well blended. Add cereal. Stir until well coated.

Press warm mixture evenly and firmly into lightly buttered 2-quart oblong glass dish. Use wax paper or buttered spatula to press firmly into an even layer. Cut into squares when cool. Yield: 24 (2-in.) squares (78 calories per square).

Total Microwave Cooking Time 3 to 4 Minutes

PROTEIN 0.7 / FAT 2.0 / CARBOHYDRATE 14.7 / SODIUM 95 / CHOLESTEROL 5

French-Style Fudge

2 ¼ cups sugar
1 (5 oz.) can evaporated milk
1 (12 oz.) pkg. semisweet chocolate chips
1 (6 oz.) pkg. milk chocolate chips
1 cup walnuts, chopped
½ cup butter
2 tablespoons vanilla

In 3-quart casserole or large glass mixing bowl, combine sugar and milk; blend well. Microwave at HIGH (10) 6 to 8 minutes until sugar is dissolved. Stir every 2 minutes. Add semisweet chocolate chips, milk chocolate chips, walnuts, butter and vanilla. Stir until thoroughly blended. Pour mixture into buttered 2-quart oblong glass dish. Refrigerate until firm. Yield: 60 pieces (102 calories per piece).

Total Microwave Cooking Time 6 to 8 Minutes

PROTEIN 0.9 / FAT 5.8 / CARBOHYDRATE 13.3 / SODIUM 21 / CHOLESTEROL 3

Peanut Brittle

1 cup sugar
½ cup light corn syrup
1 cup roasted peanuts, salted
1 teaspoon butter
1 teaspoon vanilla
1 teaspoon baking soda

In 1½-quart casserole, combine sugar and syrup. Microwave at HIGH (10) 3 minutes. Add peanuts. Microwave at HIGH (10) 4 to 5 minutes, until mixture is light brown, stirring every 2 minutes. Add butter and vanilla; stir well. Add baking soda and gently stir until light and foamy. Pour mixture onto lightly greased cookie sheet. Let cool 30 minutes to 1 hour. When cool, break into small pieces. Yield: 16 pieces (134 calories per 1 oz. piece).

Total Microwave Cooking Time 7 to 8 Minutes

PROTEIN 2.4 / FAT 4.6 / CARBOHYDRATE 21.9 / SODIUM 100 / CHOLESTEROL 0.6

Chocolate Haystacks

1 (6 oz.) pkg. semisweet
   chocolate chips
1 (3 oz.) can chow mein
   noodles

In 3-quart casserole or large bowl, place chocolate chips. Microwave at MEDIUM (5) 3½ to 5½ minutes until melted.

Stir chocolate until smooth. Add noodles. Using 2 forks, toss to coat well. On strips of foil or wax paper form into 1½-in. clusters. Cool to set. Yield: 24 clusters (52 calories each).

Note: For Butterscotch Haystacks, substitute 1 (6 oz.) pkg. butterscotch chips (1 cup) for semisweet chocolate chips.

Total Microwave Cooking Time 3½ to 5½ Minutes

PROTEIN 0.7 / FAT 3.4 / CARBOHYDRATE 6.2 / SODIUM 16 / CHOLESTEROL 0

Cherry Vanilla Bark

1 lb. vanilla flavored
   candy coating
½ cup candied cherries,
   coarsely cut

In 1-quart casserole, place candy coating. Microwave at MEDIUM (5) 4 to 7 minutes. Stir until smooth. Add cherries and mix well. Spread mixture in a thin layer on wax paper. Refrigerate until firm. Break into pieces. Yield: 1 lb. (157 calories per 1 oz. piece).

Total Microwave Cooking Time 4 to 7 Minutes

PROTEIN 1.1 / FAT 9.4 / CARBOHYDRATE 21.0 / SODIUM 14 / CHOLESTEROL 0

Chocolate Clusters

1 (6 oz.) pkg. semisweet
   chocolate chips
1 cup salted jumbo
   peanuts
1 cup seedless raisins

In a 1-quart casserole, place chocolate, peanuts and raisins. Microwave at MEDIUM HIGH (7) 2½ to 4 minutes until chocolate is melted. Stir mixture until chocolate covers peanuts and raisins. Drop by teaspoonfuls onto wax paper. Chill until firm. Yield: 20 pieces (104 calories each).

Total Microwave Cooking Time 2½ to 4 Minutes

PROTEIN 2.6 / FAT 6.3 / CARBOHYDRATE 12.1 / SODIUM 32 / CHOLESTEROL 0

Seasoning & Serving Suggestions

Herbs and spices, when used properly, add zest and flavor to almost any dish. Start by adding small amounts to your favorite recipe; taste, then increase the amount, if necessary. When cooking with fresh herbs, use three to four times more fresh herbs than dried.

The following chart is a guide for combining herbs and spices with the appropriate foods.

Herb or Spice	Breads & Cereals	Desserts	Eggs & Cheese	Fish & Shellfish
Allspice		Most fruit, cookies, spice cake		Boiled shellfish, poached fish
Basil	Noodles, pasta, rice		Cheese dishes, omelets, scrambled eggs	Crab, shrimp, tuna
Bay Leaf	Rice			Poached fish, shellfish
Caraway Seeds	Pumpernickel and rye bread		Cottage cheese, mild cheese	Tuna casserole
Celery Seed	Stuffing for meat, poultry or fish		Cheese dishes	Baked or broiled fish
Cinnamon	Hot cereals	Fresh fruit, cookies, puddings, fruit pies	Cottage cheese, French toast	
Cloves	Coffee cakes, sweet rolls, quick breads	Fresh fruit, gingerbread, pumpkin pie, spice cake, fruit cake		Baked or broiled fish
Curry Powder	Rice, corn bread	Fruit compotes	Deviled eggs	Shrimp, seafood salad
Dill	Pumpernickel and rye bread		Cottage cheese, deviled eggs	Baked, broiled or grilled fish
Ginger	Quick breads	Cookies, fresh fruit, puddings, pumpkin pie, gingerbread		Oriental stir-fries
Marjoram	Biscuits, stuffing for poultry and fish		Cheese dishes, omelets, scrambled eggs	Baked or broiled fish
Mustard			Cheese dishes, deviled eggs	Deviled crab, fish, shellfish
Nutmeg	Rice	Custard, fresh fruit, rice pudding, stewed prunes, banana cake	Scrambled eggs	Fish casseroles
Oregano	Pasta, meat and poultry stuffing, lasagna		Cheese dishes, omelets, scrambled eggs	Shellfish
Rosemary	Corn bread, poultry stuffing		Cheese dishes, omelets, scrambled eggs	Baked or broiled fish
Sage	Pork and poultry stuffing		Cottage cheese	Baked or broiled fish
Tarragon	Poultry stuffing		Egg dishes	Baked or broiled fish
Thyme	Dumplings, fish and poultry stuffings		Cheese dishes, omelets, scrambled eggs	Baked or broiled fish, shellfish

Meats	Poultry	Sauces & Marinades	Soups & Stews	Vegetables
Baked ham, meat loaf, pot roast		Barbecue sauce, beef marinades, cranberry sauce, tomato sauce	Asparagus, pea and vegetable soups, beef or chicken stew	Beets, carrots, sweet potatoes, turnips, winter squash
Beef, lamb, meat loaf, pork	Chicken	Spaghetti sauce, tomato sauce	Bean, potato and vegetable soups, beef stew	Broccoli, eggplant, green beans, summer squash, tomatoes
Beef, lamb, pot roast		Gravy, meat marinades	Chowder, chicken, pea and vegetable soups, most stews	Beets, carrots, green beans, onions, summer squash, tomatoes
Pork roast		Cheese sauce, meat marinades	Beef stew, seafood stew	Asparagus, cabbage, mushrooms, sauerkraut, turnips
Meat loaf	Chicken, turkey	Cream sauces	Chicken soup, vegetable soup, most stews	Cabbage, mushrooms, onion, tomatoes
Lamb chops, pork chops	Chicken	Applesauce, fruit dessert sauces	Fruit soups, beef or lamb stew	Beets, carrots, sweet potatoes, winter squash
Baked ham, roast pork		Meat marinades, tomato sauce	Bean, potato and split pea soups, borscht, fruit soups	Beets, carrots, sweet potatoes, winter squash
Beef, pork, lamb	Chicken, turkey	Teriyaki sauce, cream sauce		Carrots, tomatoes, onions
Lamb chops, veal	Chicken	Cocktail sauce, sauces for fish	Beef or lamb stew	Cabbage, cauliflower, green beans, potatoes
Hawaiian dishes, Oriental stir-fries, pot roast, veal	Oriental stir-fries, roasted chicken	Teriyaki sauce, fish marinades	Bean, onion and potato soups, most stews	Beets, carrots, sweet potatoes, winter squash
Lamb, pork, roast beef, veal	Chicken, turkey		Chicken and vegetable soups, most stews	Carrots, eggplant, lima beans, peas, spinach, tomatoes
Hamburgers, hash, lamb, meat loaf, beef	Chicken	Barbecue sauce, meat marinades, sauces for vegetables	Bean soup, cream soups, lentil soup	Beets, cabbage, sauerkraut
Beef, meat loaf	Creamed chicken	Cream sauces	Chicken soup, cream soups	Carrots, green beans, spinach, squash, sweet potatoes
Beef, lamb, meat loaf, meatballs, pizza, pork, pot roast	Chicken	Gravy, spaghetti sauce	Tomato and vegetable soups, beef stew, chili	Dry beans, eggplant, green beans, potatoes, spinach, tomatoes, zucchini
Beef, lamb, pork, veal	Chicken, turkey		Chicken, pea and spinach soups	Cauliflower, peas, potatoes, summer squash, turnips
Pork	Chicken, turkey		Chicken soup, chowder, cream soup, vegetable soup	Eggplant, lima beans, onions
Lamb	Chicken, turkey	Sauces for fish		Tomatoes
Beef, lamb, pork	Chicken, turkey	Sauces for fish	Clam chowder, beef and poultry stews	Dry beans, carrots, eggplant, green beans, mushrooms, peas, spinach, tomatoes, zucchini

Microwaving Guide

1. Refer to the chart below when microwaving raw or uncooked foods.
2. Since microwaving does not brown food as in conventional cooking, you may prefer to cook foods such as meats and baked goods in a conventional oven.
3. Always cook in microwave-safe plastic or glass utensils. Paper is acceptable for some foods. *DO NOT USE METAL CONTAINERS.*

4. When covering utensils with plastic wrap, turn back one corner to vent.
5. Cooktimes and food quantities given should be used as a guide. In microwaving, the greater the quantity of food the longer time it will take to cook.

FOOD		Cover	Power Level and Time	Comments
Appetizers	Party mix (2½-quarts)	No	High (10) 5 to 7 minutes.	Stir every 2 minutes.
	Meatballs, small meat or hot dog chunks (24)	Wax paper or plastic wrap	High (10) 5 to 8 minutes.	Spread in single layer in 2-quart oblong glass baking dish.
	Stuffed vegetables (12)	No	High (10) 3 to 5 minutes.	Space evenly on trivet or on plate lined with paper towels.
	Toasted nuts or seeds (½ to 1 cup)	No	High (10) 3 to 5 minutes.	Combine nuts with small amount of butter, stirring every 2 minutes.
Cakes, Cookies, Breads	Oblong, square or round cake	No	High (10) 2 minutes. Medium High (7) 3 to 5 minutes.	
	Fluted tube cake	No	High (10) 12 to 16 minutes.	Let stand 5 to 10 minutes before inverting.
	Cheesecake (9-inch pie plate)	No	Medium High (7) 10 to 14 minutes.	Microwave cheesecake mixture in 2-quart casserole until thick and smooth. Stir every 2 minutes with wire whisk. Pour into crumb crust. Refrigerate until firm.
	Bar Cookies (8-in. square dish)	No	High (10) 5 to 7 minutes.	Rotate ½ turn after 3 minutes.
	Muffins (6)	No	Medium High (7) 2 to 4 minutes.	Check at minimum time.
Eggs, Cheese, Dairy	Scrambled eggs	No	High (10) ¾ to 1 minute per egg.	Stir 2 or 3 times during microwaving.
	Quiche	No	Medium High (7) 15 to 21 minutes.	Pour filling into prebaked shell.
	Thickened sauces and gravies (1 cup)	No	Medium (5) 3 to 5 minutes.	Microwave fat, flour and salt 1 to 2 minutes; stir to blend. Add liquid. Stir every minute.
	Scald milk (½ cup)	No	Medium High (7) 3 to 5 minutes.	
	Melt butter (½ cup)	No	High (10) ½ to 1 minute.	
	Soften cream cheese (8 oz.)	No	Low (3) ½ to 1 minute.	Remove foil wrapper and place on microwave-safe plate.
Fish & Shellfish	Fillets or steaks (1 lb.)	Wax paper	High (10) 5 to 7 minutes.	Very delicate fish should be placed on trivet.
	Casserole, pre-cooked (2 to 3 quart)	Plastic wrap	High (10) 12 to 18 minutes.	
	Scallops, shrimp, peeled (1 lb.)	Plastic wrap	High (10) 4 to 7 minutes.	Brush with garlic butter before cooking.
Fruits	Baked apples or pears	Lid or plastic wrap	High (10) 2 to 4 minutes per piece.	Pierce fruit or peel to prevent bursting.

FOOD		Cover	Power Level and Time	Comments
Meat	Ground meat (1 lb.)	Lid or wax paper	High (10) 5 to 7 minutes.	Break up and stir every 2 minutes.
	Bacon (2 to 8 strips)	Paper towels	High (10) ¾ to 1 minute per slice.	Place on trivet or paper towel-lined plate.
	Sausage	Wax paper	High (10) Patties: 1 minute per patty. Links: ½ to ¾ minute per link.	Place on paper towel-lined plate or glass dish. Turn over after half of cooking time.
	Franks or hot dogs (1 lb.)	Lid or wax paper	High (10) 3 to 6 minutes.	Add ⅓ cup water. Rearrange after half of cooking time.
	Meat casseroles with pre-cooked meat and ingredients	Lid or plastic wrap	High (10) 19 to 30 minutes.	Stir once or twice.
	Meat stews with raw meat and vegetables	Lid or plastic wrap	Medium (5) 70 to 80 minutes.	Rearrange or stir after half time.
	Meat patties (4 per lb.)	Wax paper	High (10) 5 to 7 minutes.	Place on trivet or on paper towel-lined plate. Rearrange patties after 3 minutes.
	Meat loaf, beef or ham (1½ lbs. meat)	Plastic wrap	Medium High (7) 25 to 28 minutes.	
	Spareribs (2 to 3 lbs.)	Lid or plastic wrap	Medium (5) 80 to 90 minutes.	Cover meat with water. Rearrange after half of cooking time. Drain 10 minutes before end of cooking time; add barbecue sauce and complete cooking.
	Chops with sauce (4 1-inch chops)	Wax paper	Medium High (7) 30 to 40 minutes.	Turn over after half of cooking time.
Pasta & Cereals	Long pieces (spaghetti, etc, ½ lb.)	Plastic wrap	High (10) 12 to 15 minutes.	In 2-quart oblong glass dish, add 6 cups hot tap water, 1 tablespoon oil, 1 teaspoon salt. Rearrange after half of cooking time.
	Noodle or rice casseroles (2 quarts)	Lid or plastic wrap	High (10) 8 to 15 minutes.	Stir after ½ of cooking time. Add topping just before serving.
	Cereal or instant rice	Lid or plastic wrap	High (10) 1½ to 3 minutes per serving.	Add amount of hot tap water given on package. Stir after half of cooking time.
Pies	Crumb crust (9-inch)	No	Medium (5) 2 to 3 minutes.	Rotate dish ½ turn after 1 minute.
Poultry	Chicken, 6 to 8 pieces	Wax paper or plastic wrap	High (10) 11 to 16 minutes.	
	Whole chicken or Cornish hens	Cooking Bag	Medium High (7) 9 to 12 minutes per lb.	Turn over after half of cooking time.
	Turkey legs or quarters	Cooking Bag	Medium (5) 11 to 14 minutes per lb.	Turn over after half of cooking time.
	Turkey breast	Cooking Bag	Medium (5) 12 to 15 minutes per lb.	Place on trivet, breast side down. Turn over after half of cooking time.
Roasts	Pot roast 3 to 4 lbs.)	Cooking Bag	Medium (5) 18 to 23 minutes per lb.	Turn over after half of cooking time.
	Tender beef roast (rib-eye, bone-in rib, rolled rib)	Cooking Bag	Medium (5) Rare: 11 to 14 minutes per lb. Medium: 14 to 17 minutes per lb. Well done: 17 to 20 minutes per lb.	Turn over after half of cooking time.
	Pork roast	Cooking Bag	Medium (5) 13 to 18 minutes per lb.	Turn over after half of cooking time.
	Ham roast, pre-cooked	Cooking Bag	Medium (5) 14 to 17 minutes per lb.	Turn over after half of cooking time.

Defrosting Chart *Power Level: Defrost (3)*

1. Most foods defrost well using Defrost (3). For more even defrosting of larger beef, lamb and veal roasts use Warm (1).
2. Most foods should be turned over or rearranged after half of defrosting time.

3. When defrosting steaks or chops, separate and remove defrosted pieces after half of defrost time. Allow these portions to stand on counter to complete defrosting and return frozen pieces to oven to complete defrosting.

FOOD		First Half Time, Min.	Second Half Time, Min.	Comments
Breads, Cakes	Bread or buns (1-lb. pkg.)	2	1 to 2	Turn over after first half of time.
	Heat & serve rolls (7-oz. pkg.)	1	1 to 2	
	Coffee cake (11 to 13 oz.)	2	2 to 4	
	Coffee ring (10-oz. pkg.)	2	1 to 2	
	Sweet rolls (12-oz. pkg.)	1½	1 to 2	
	Doughnuts (1 to 3)	½ to 1	none	
	Doughnuts, glazed (box of 12)	1	1 to 2	
	French toast (2 slices)	1½	1 to 1½	
	Cake, frosted 2 to 3 layer (17 oz.)	3	none	Let stand 5 to 10 minutes before serving.
	Cake, filled or topped 1 layer (12½ to 16 oz.)	1	1 to 2	Let stand 5 to 10 minutes before serving.
	Pound cake (11¼ oz.)	2 to 4	none	Let stand 5 to 10 minutes before serving.
	Cheesecake, plain or fruit top (17 to 19 oz.)	2	1 to 2	
	Crunch cakes & cupcakes (1 to 2)	½ to 1	none	
	Fruit or nut pie (8 inch)	4	3 to 6	
	Cream or custard pie (14 oz.)	1	1 to 2	
Fish & Seafood	Fillets (1 lb.)	4 to 5	5 to 7	Place unopened package in oven. (If fish is frozen in water, place in cooking dish.) After second half of time, hold under cold waster to separate.
	Steaks (6 oz.)	2	1	Place wrapped steaks in oven.
	Whole fish (8 to 10 oz.)	2	3 to 4	Place fish in cooking dish. Turn over after first half of time. After second half of time, rinse cavity with cold water to complete defrosting.
	Shellfish, small pieces (1 lb.)	3 to 4	2 to 4	Spread shellfish in single layer in baking dish. Rearrange pieces after first half of time.
	Shellfish, blocks Crab meat (6-oz. pkg.)	2	2 to 3	Place block in casserole. Turn over and break up with fork after first half of time.
	Oysters (12-oz. carton)	5 to 7	5 to 7	Place block in casserole. Turn over and break up with fork after first half of time.
	Scallops (1-lb. pkg.)	5 to 7	5 to 7	Place block in casserole. Turn over and break up with fork after first half of time.
	Shellfish, large Crab legs – 1 to 2 (8 to 10 oz.)	2 to 3	2 to 3	Arrange in cooking dish with light underside up. Turn over after first half of time.
	Lobster tails – 1 to 2 (6 to 9 oz.)	3 to 4	3 to 4	Arrange in cooking dish with light underside up. Turn over after first half of time.

FOOD		First Half Time, Min.	Second Half Time, Min.	Comments
Fruit	Fresh (10 to 16 oz.) (In microwave-safe container)	2 ½	1 to 2	Place package in oven. After first half of time, break up with fork. Let stand on counter to complete defrosting.
	Plastic pouch — 1 to 2 (10-oz. pkg.)	2 ½	1 to 3	Place package in oven. After first half of time, flex package.
Meat	Bacon (1 lb.)	2 to 3 per lb.	1 to 2 per lb.	Place unopened package in oven. Turn over after first half of time. Microwave just until strips can be separated.
	Franks (1 lb.) (½ lb.)	1 to 2 / 1 ½ to 2 ½	1 to 2 / none	Place unopened package in oven. Turn over after first half of time. Microwave just until franks can be separated.
	Ground beef or pork (1 lb.)	5	2 to 4	Scrape off meat that softens during defrosting. Set aside. Break up remaining block and continue defrosting.
	(1 ½ to 2 lbs.)	7	7	Scrape off meat that softens during defrosting. Set aside. Break up remaining block and continue defrosting.
	(5 lbs.)	13	13	Scrape off meat that softens during defrosting. Set aside. Break up remaining block and continue defrosting.
	Roast: beef, lamb or veal (3 to 5 lbs.)	Use Warm (1) for roasts 7 per lb.	6 to 7 per lb.	Place unwrapped roast in glass casserole. Turn over after first half of time. Let stand 30 minutes.
	Roast, pork (3 to 5 lbs.)	4 to 5 per lb.	4 to 5 per lb.	Place unwrapped roast in glass casserole. Turn over after first half of time. Let stand 30 minutes.
	Spareribs, pork (1 ½ lbs.)	2 to 4 per lb.	2 to 4 per lb.	Place wrapped package in oven. Turn over after first half of time; unwrap and separate pieces. Let stand to complete defrosting.
	Steaks, chops or cutlets (beef, lamb, pork or veal)	3 to 5 per lb.	2 to 5 per lb.	Place wrapped package in oven. Turn over after first half of time; unwrap and separate pieces. Let stand to complete defrosting.
	Sausage, bulk (1-lb. roll)	2 to 3	2 to 3	Scrape off softened meat after first half of time. Set aside. Break up remaining block, and continue defrosting.
	Sausage, link (½ to 1 lb.)	1 ½	1 to 2	Turn over after first half of time.
	Sausage, patties (12-oz. pkg.)	2	1 to 3	Turn over and separate after first half of time.
Poultry	Chicken, cut up (2 ½ to 3 ½ lbs.)	7 to 8	7 to 8	Place wrapped chicken in oven. After first half of time, unwrap, turn over and separate pieces. Place in cooking dish and finish defrosting.
	Chicken, whole (2 ½ to 3 ½ lbs.)	10 to 12	10 to 12	Place wrapped chicken in oven. After first half of time unwrap and turn over. Shield warm areas with foil.
	Cornish hen	5 to 6 per lb.	5 to 6 per lb.	Place wrapped package in oven. Turn over after first half of time; unwrap and shield warm areas with foil.
	Duckling	4 to 6 per lb.	4 to 6 per lb.	Place wrapped duckling in oven. After first half of time, unwrap, turn over and place in cooking dish. Shield warm areas with foil.
	Turkey breast	3 to 5 per lb.	3 to 5 per lb.	Place unwrapped turkey, breast side down, in cooking dish. After first half of time, turn turkey breast side up and shield warm areas with foil.

Heating or Reheating Chart

1. Refer to the chart below for reheating cooked foods at refrigerator or room temperature. Use microwave oven-safe containers.
2. Cover most foods for fastest heating. When covering with plastic wrap, turn back one corner to vent.
3. Bubbling around edges of dish is normal, since center is last to heat. Stir foods before serving whenever possible.
4. Stir or rearrange large amounts of food after half the suggested heating time.

5. Be sure foods are heated through before serving. Steaming or bubbling around edges does not necessarily mean food is heated throughout. As a general rule, hot foods produce an area warm to the touch in center of underside of dish.
6. To be thoroughly heated, food should reach a temperature of 160°F to 165°F. Allow foods to stand a few minutes before serving.

Item		Amount	Power Level	Approx. Time, Minutes
Appetizers	Saucy: meatballs, riblets, cocktail franks, etc. ½ cup / serving	1 to 2 servings 3 to 4 servings	High (10) High (10)	1 to 2 3 to 4
	Dips: cream or process cheese	½ cup 1 cup	Medium (5) Medium (5)	½ to 1 2 to 3
	Pastry bites: small pizzas, egg rolls etc.	2 to 4 servings	High (10)	1 to 3
	Tip: Cover saucy appetizers with wax paper. Cover dips with plastic wrap. Do not cover pastry bites.			
Plate of Leftovers	Meat plus 2 vegetables	1 to 2 plates	High (10)	2 to 4
	Tip: Cover plate of food with wax paper or plastic wrap.			
Meats & Main Dishes	Saucy Main Dishes: chop suey, spaghetti, creamed chicken, chili, stew, macaroni and cheese, etc. ¾ to 1 cup / serving	1 to 2 servings 3 to 4 servings 1 16-oz. can	High (10) High (10) High (10)	1 to 2 2 to 3 2 to 3
	Thinly sliced roasted meat: Rare, minimum time Medium Rare, maximum time 3 to 4 oz. / serving	1 to 2 servings 3 to 4 servings	Medium High (7) Medium High (7)	1 to 3 2 to 4
	Well done beef, pork, ham, poultry, etc. 3 to 4 oz. / serving	1 to 2 servings 3 to 4 servings	Medium High (7) Medium High (7)	1 to 3 3 to 4
	Steaks, chops, ribs, other meat pieces:			
	Rare beef steak	1 to 2 servings 3 to 4 servings	Medium High (7) Medium High (7)	1 to 2 2 to 3
	Well done beef, chops, ribs, etc.	1 to 2 servings 4 servings	Medium High (7) Medium High (7)	1 to 2 2 to 3
	Hamburgers or meat loaf 4 oz. / serving	1 to 2 servings 3 to 4 servings	High (10) High (10)	1 to 1½ 2 to 3
	Chicken pieces	1 to 2 pieces 3 to 4 pieces	High (10) High (10)	1 to 1½ 2 to 3
	Hot dogs and sausages	1 to 2 3 to 4	High (10) High (10)	½ to 1½ 1½ to 2
	Rice and pasta Plain or buttered ½ to 1 cup / serving	1 to 2 servings 3 to 4 servings	High (10) High (10)	1 to 2 2 to 3
	Topped or mixed with sauce ½ to 1 cup / serving	1 to 2 servings 3 to 4 servings	High (10) High (10)	1 to 2 2 to 4
	Tip: Cover saucy main dishes with plastic wrap. Cover other main dishes and meats with wax paper. Do not cover rare or medium rare meats.			

Item		Amount	Power Level	Approx. Time, Minutes
Sandwiches & Soups	Moist filling:			
	sloppy joe, barbecue, ham salad, etc. in bun	1 to 2 servings	Medium High (7)	1 to 2
	⅓ cup / serving	3 to 4 servings	Medium High (7)	2 to 4
	Meat-cheese filling with firm bread	1 to 2 servings	Medium High (7)	1 to 1½
		3 to 4 servings	Medium High (7)	1½ to 2½
	Soup			
	Water based 1 cup / serving	1 to 2 servings	High (10)	1 to 3
		3 to 4 servings	High (10)	3 to 4
		1 10-oz. can reconstituted	High (10)	3 to 4
	Milk based 1 cup / serving	1 to 2 servings	Medium High (7)	2 to 3
		3 to 4 servings	Medium High (7)	3 to 5
		1 10-oz. can reconstituted	Medium High (7)	6 to 8

Tip: Use paper towel or napkin to cover sandwiches. Cover soups with wax paper or plastic wrap.

Item		Amount	Power Level	Approx. Time, Minutes
Vegetables	Small pieces			
	peas, bean, corn, etc.	1 to 2 servings	High (10)	1 to 2
	½ cup / serving	3 to 4 servings	High (10)	2 to 3
		1 16-oz. can	High (10)	2 to 3
	Large pieces or whole	1 to 2 servings	High (10)	1 to 2
	asparagus spears, corn on the cob, etc.	3 to 4 servings	High (10)	2 to 3
		1 16-oz. can	High (10)	2 to 3
	Mashed potatoes, squash, pumpkin, etc.	1 to 2 servings	High (10)	1 to 2
	½ cup / serving	3 to 4 servings	High (10)	3 to 4

Tip: Cover vegetables for most even heating.

Item		Amount	Power Level	Approx. Time, Minutes
Sauces	Dessert: chocolate or butterscotch	½ cup	High (10)	½ to 1
		1 cup	High (10)	1 to 2
	Meat or main dish, chunky type	½ cup	High (10)	½ to 1
	giblet gravy, spaghetti sauce, etc.	1 cup	High (10)	1 to 2
		1 16-oz. can	High (10)	2 to 3
	Creamy type	½ cup	High (10)	½ to 1
		1 cup	High (10)	1 to 2

Tip: Cover food to prevent spatter.

Item		Amount	Power Level	Approx. Time, Minutes
Bakery Foods	Cake, coffee cake, doughnuts, sweet rolls, nut or fruit bread	1 piece	Low (3)	½ to 1
		2 pieces	Low (3)	1 to 1½
		9-in. cake or 12 rolls or doughnuts	Low (3)	2 to 4
	Dinner rolls, muffins	1	Medium (5)	¼ to ½
		2 to 4	Medium (5)	½ to 1
		6 to 8	Medium (5)	1 to 2
	Pie fruit, nut or custard	1 slice	High (10)	½ to 1
	⅛ of 9-in. pie = 1 slice	2 slices	High (10)	1 to 1½
	(use minimum time for custard)	9-in. pie	Medium High (7)	3 to 4

Item		Amount	Power Level	Approx. Time, Minutes
Griddle Foods	Pancakes, French toast or waffles			
	Plain, no topping	2 or 3 pieces	High (10)	½ to 1
	With syrup & butter	2 or 3 pieces	High (10)	1 to 2
	With 2 sausage patties (cooked)	2 or 3 pieces	High (10)	1 to 2

Item		Amount	Power Level	Approx. Time, Minutes
Beverages	Coffee, tea, cider, other water based	1 to 2 cups	High (10)	1 to 3
		3 to 4 cups	High (10)	4 to 6
	Cocoa, other milk based	1 to 2 cups	Medium High (7)	3 to 4
		3 to 4 cups	Medium High (7)	5 to 6

Index

Index

Index

CREDITS:
Wendy Shafer Shirrell
Brigid Lally Bowles
Joyce Lose Effinger
Cynthia Fanning Forester

Consumer Information
Testing Laboratory
GE Appliances

Design, Production, Photography and Food Styling:
OTT Communications, Inc.
Louisville, Kentucky